TOO GOOD TO BE TRUE?

How we get to Heaven
  What it will be like
    And why we can't live without it

Too Good to be True?

Copyright © 2016 by James Rochford

Unless otherwise identified, all scripture quotations in this publication are from the *New American Standard Bible* (NASB), © The Lockman Foundation 1960, 1962, 1963, 1968, 1971, 1972, 1973, 1975, 1977.

Visit http://www.xenos.org for bulk orders and author access

International Standard Book Number

Cover design by Ian Adams

New Paradigm Publishing
Columbus, OH

Table of Contents

Chapter 1: Something is missing

Do you ever get the feeling that something is missing?

Advertisers claim to have the answer, clamoring endlessly like a friend who had too much to drink. Commercials capitalize on the sense that we're missing something: a bigger house, a nicer car, smoother skin, tighter abs, or a firmer butt. Yet we never quite feel fulfilled—or filled full—by such things. At least, not for long. Even after a string of purchases that vague sense of emptiness sets in.

Something is missing, *but what?* We might yearn for the ecstasy of romance, but when the thrill is gone, we feel even lonelier than before. We cycle through relationships like a merry-go-round, but when the music stops, we don't feel "merry." Even when we're engulfed by the loud music of a night club or the laughter of a party, a fleeting feeling of alienation returns. (It's surprising how lonely we can feel even in such crowded places!)

Henry David Thoreau once wrote, "The mass of men lead lives of quiet desperation… Unconscious despair is concealed even under what are called the games and amusements of mankind."[1] The term "a-muse" literally means "not thinking," and amusement has only multiplied since Thoreau wrote these words in 1854. Instead of quiet reflection, we prefer the stimulation of a flat screen; rather than sitting in silence, we reach for our headphones; and in

---

[1] Henry David Thoreau, *Walden* (New York: Thomas Y. Crowell & Co., 1910), 8.

the place of intimate conversation, we multiply friendships on social media.

As we grow older, we reminisce about old friends and family—periods of life claimed by the past. As children grow up and move out, we're left with a quiet house and our memories. What was once a roaring fire becomes a mound of embers and finally ashes.

Some people deny that anything is missing in their lives. Of course, no one can force you to admit something is missing. The old adage still rings true: "A man convinced against his will is of the same opinion still." But I would ask you a very simple question:

Really…?

Are you *really* satisfied with your life and the decisions you've made? Are you *really* content with your relationships and how they've turned out? Is another promotion or another purchase *really* the answer? Will a change of ZIP code *really* change everything? At the very least, we can look to innumerable people who have had all of their earthly desires fulfilled, yet still yearned for *more*.

> **Eric Clapton (musician):** "I had everything a man could want even then. I was a millionaire. I had beautiful women in my life. I had cars. A house. An incredible, solid-gold career. And a future. And yet, on a day-to-day basis, I wanted to commit suicide."[2]

> **Tom Brady (NFL quarterback with four Super Bowl rings):** "[Why do I] still think there is

---

[2] Eric Clapton, interview with *VH1* (1999).

something greater out there for me? ...I think, 'God, there's got to be more than this!'"[3]

Halle Berry (actress): "Beauty is essentially meaningless, and it is always transitory."[4]

Josh Radnor (actor, *How I Met Your Mother*): "I had bought into the not-uncommon notion that when I taste success, when I get 'over there,' then I'll be happy. But the strangest thing happened: As the show got more successful, I got more depressed."[5]

John Lennon (musician): "As a 'Beatle,' we made it, and there was nothing to do. We had money. We had fame. And there was no joy."[6]

Cameron Diaz (actress): "If you are looking for fame to define you, then you will never be happy. You will always be searching for happiness. You will never find it in fame."[7]

Tony Hale (actor, *Arrested Development*): "I kept thinking, 'Oh that sitcom is coming...' And when I got it... I mean, I won't say it was a *depression*, but you kind of go through a *disappointment*. Because that fame didn't satisfy the way you thought it was going to satisfy."[8]

Russell Brand (actor, comedian): "I thought [that] it would be good to be rich and famous... It would be

[3] Tom Brady, interview with Steve Kroft *60 Minutes* (2005).

[4] Stephen M. Silverman "Halle Berry: Beauty Can't Stop Heartache" *People Magazine*, (August 03, 2004).

[5] Josh Radnor, INKtalk (October, 2015).

[6] John Lennon, interview (https://www.youtube.com/watch?v=Yd9m4corSLw).

[7] Cameron Diaz, *HUMAN* interview (2015).

[8] Tony Hale, interview with Paul F. Tompkins on "Speakeasy" (2013).

good to have money, it would be good to be invited to the party. Well, I've been invited… I've seen the other side of the looking glass, and it ain't… worth it. It [doesn't] fill your soul. I still feel empty inside."[9]

Are you determined to find fulfillment in the pleasures of this world? Good luck. You're pursuing a goal that has never been achieved by the billions of people before you. You'll never find it, because there's nothing to find.

Do you know what Jesus' first words were in the gospel according to John? He asked this question: *"What do you seek?"* (Jn. 1:38) Two thousand years later, those haunting words still confront us. What exactly am I looking for? What do I want? Fame? Money? Power? A new car? A bigger house or a nicer spouse? What will finally satisfy my soul?

Perhaps you've been going about this search all wrong. Maybe you've been looking for fulfillment in the wrong places, or possibly, in the wrong place. What if this world will never satisfy you, because you were made for another world altogether?

Is there life after death?

Modern medicine continues to astound us. We live in an age of bionic limbs, viral vaccinations, skin grafts, and heart transplants. Yet despite our scientific progress, humanity still has a 100 percent mortality rate—no one is getting out of here alive. We might live for eighteen years or eighty, but death remains a certainty.

But is there something *after* death?

---

[9] Russell Brand, interview with Mehdi Hasan "A Brand New Politics," (2013).

Our earliest ancestors surely thought so, placing flowers in the graves of their dead.[10] One grave dating to ~25,000 years ago contains the bodies of two children, laid head to head, with their hands placed gently over their pelvises. Anthropologists tell us that the 250 fox teeth and 5,000 ivory beads adorning their small bodies must have taken around 2,500 hours to create.[11] While we don't know much about our ancient ancestors, we do know this: they spent considerable time, talent, and treasure on their funerals.

According to the authoritative *Encyclopedia of Religion and Ethics*, even the oldest and most primitive human cultures believed in the afterlife:

> No subject... has so engrossed the mind of man as that of his condition after death.... There is every reason to believe that they regarded the dead as still carrying on some kind of existence.... [Primitive people] had thought much about it.... There are very few [primitive] peoples who believe in utter extinction.[12]

Millennia later, modern people still walk in their footsteps. Belief in life after death persists in virtually every culture and civilization on Earth. Scholar Alan Segel writes, "Most, if not all, of the world's cultures maintain some sort of belief

---

[10] Philip Lieberman, *Uniquely Human: the Evolution of Speech, Thought, and Selfless Behavior* (Cambridge, MA: Harvard UP, 1993), 162-164.

[11] Paul Pettitt, *The Palaeolithic Origins of Human Burial* (New York, Routledge, 2011), 198-207.

[12] MacCulloch, J.A. *Encyclopedia of Religion and Ethics*, "State of the Dead." (Edinburgh: T. & T. Clark), 1981, 817-819.

in life after death."[13] In fact, even amid modern skepticism, three out of four Americans continue to believe in Heaven.[14]

We might wonder why so many people from so many different cultures and eras of history would believe in life after death. After all, the afterlife cannot be empirically tested or scientifically proven—so why do so many people believe in it?

Humanity's hope isn't the result of a collective delusion or an anthropological abnormality. Such explanations don't *explain* this phenomenon; instead, they attempt to *explain it away*. The Bible tells us, "[God] has planted eternity in the human heart" (Eccl. 3:11 NLT). This is the real explanation for why humans have always believed in an afterlife, and if true, it means nothing in this world will ever ultimately satisfy us. We were made for another world: Heaven.

The denial of death

Nothing is more certain than death, but oddly, nothing is more strange or shocking. For such a normal process, death still feels so abnormal—so wrong. Psychologist Frederic Neuman observes,

> There is something about death. In an odd way death seems unnatural—uncanny, almost, because it is so far outside our experience. And so abrupt... Even when a woman is 93 years old, and has been dying for months, her death seems sudden... When that person is loved, and needed, death always

---

[13] Alan F. Segal, *Life after Death: a History of the Afterlife in the Religions of the West* (New York: Doubleday, 2004), 18.
[14] *The Pew Forum on Religion and Public Life*. "US Religious Landscape Survey." February, 2008. 168.

> seems premature. And unexpected. So, it seems to
> me sometimes that no one dies a natural death.[15]

The grisly certainty of death drives many people in Western culture to avoid the subject altogether. Even our language tries to camouflage this gruesome reality: We don't place our dead in *coffins* anymore, but in *caskets*; we no longer send our dead to *morgues*, but to *funeral homes*; in fact, instead of *dying*, our loved ones merely *pass away* or *depart*.

Of course, we can change our vocabulary all we want, but death doesn't change. Death doesn't pay attention to our softened synonyms or even our outright denial. Death stalks each one of us—undeterred. No matter how much the mortician manicures and perfumes the body of our loved one, he doesn't have the power to bring him or her back to life.

So what should we make of death? Should we merely "make friends with the necessity of dying"[16] as some atheistic thinkers have argued? *Not at all!* Death is an enemy of the human race—not a friend. The Bible tells us that "the last enemy that will be abolished is death" (1 Cor. 15:26), and Jesus "set free all who have lived their lives as slaves to the fear of dying" (Heb. 2:15 NLT). Jesus tells us, "I hold the keys of death" (Rev. 1:18 NIV) and, "I am the resurrection and the life; he who believes in Me will live even if he dies" (Jn. 11:25). Death could not hold Jesus in its powerful grip (Acts 2:24), and it will not hold us either.

---

[15] Dr. Frederic Neuman. "It Seems No One Ever Dies a Natural Death." *Psychology Today*. February 19, 2013.

[16] Sigmund Freud, "The Theme of the Three Caskets." *The Standard Edition of the Complete Psychological Works of Sigmund Freud, Volume XII (1911-1913)* (London: Vintage Books, 1913), 300.

Jesus is the only person who knows how to get to Heaven, because he is the only one who has ever "come down from Heaven" (Jn. 6:38); and according to him, this life is not the end—only the beginning. A split second after you die, you stand face to face with your Creator.

And then, eternal life will begin.

The average American lives about 78 years. But many live that entire time without knowing what their purpose is, or where they're going when their time is up. One of the wisest men who ever lived once wrote, "A wise person thinks a lot about death, while a fool thinks only about having a good time" (Eccl. 7:4). Wouldn't it be worth spending a couple of hours to read this book and explore what your life is all about?

Chapter 2: Do good people go to Heaven?

Many intelligent, educated, and accomplished people from all over the world believe in life after death, but they haven't thought about how they'll get there.

Isn't that odd? We might spend eighty years on Earth, but we'll spend *eternity* someplace else. If life after death exists, wouldn't it be worth discovering what it will be like? Shouldn't we seek some sort of assurance for where we're headed?

Let's say you were travelling to the Bahamas, but you were intent on flying there without any security clearance, a photo I.D., or even a ticket.[1] My friend, you wouldn't make it past the first metal detector! And if you didn't give up your endeavor, you'd be spending your vacation basking beneath the fluorescent lights of the local jail, rather than in the tropical sun.

Of course, this scenario is utterly ridiculous, but that's exactly the point: who would ever be so presumptuous? Surely we would never travel to another country without preparing a plan, or at the very least, carrying a passport. Yet many expect to travel from this world to the next one without any forethought whatsoever.

---

[1] I am indebted to Greg Laurie for this illustration. Greg Laurie, *As It Is In Heaven: How Eternity Brings Focus to What Really Matters* (Colorado Springs, CO: NavPress, 2014), 41.

A popular theory about the afterlife has convinced many people that they will live forever in Heaven. Different people express this view in different ways, but the core belief goes something like this: "Good people go to Heaven. Bad people go to Hell." Have you heard this view before, or do you hold this theory yourself? Don't worry. You're not alone. Many people are banking their eternities on this idea about the afterlife.

But as odd as it might sound, the Bible nowhere teaches this perspective.

Pretty good or perfection?

In ancient Israel, the Jewish people revered the scribes and Pharisees as the pinnacle of piety and perfection. So it must have surprised these people to hear Jesus say, "Unless your righteousness *surpasses* that of the scribes and Pharisees, you will not enter the kingdom of heaven" (Mt. 5:20).

And just as they were picking their jaws up off the floor, Jesus went on to say, "You are to be perfect, as your heavenly Father is perfect" (Mt. 5:48). Imagine that! God doesn't grade on a curve. He demands a standard of unqualified moral perfection. Jesus' closest followers only confirmed his teaching: committing even *one* sin will spoil our moral standing before God.

> Whoever keeps the whole law and yet stumbles in one point, he has become guilty of all. (Jas. 2:10)

> Those who depend on the law to make them right with God are under his curse, for the Scriptures say, 'Cursed is everyone who does not observe and obey

all the commands that are written in God's Book of the Law.' (Gal. 3:10 NLT)

I still remember going to the public pool as a kid. One hot summer day, I had just entered the water when the lifeguard blew her whistle, because someone had defecated in the pool. Once we saw the small and smelly "submarine" floating across the surface of the water, I don't recall anyone saying, "Hey, let's just move down to the deep end... Nobody pooped down there!" Instead everyone had to get out, ruining our afternoon. Even though the pool was *mostly* filled with chlorinated water, it was still *completely* soiled by one person's lack of bowel control.

Similarly, even one sin completely contaminates us before God. Like a small cluster of cancer cells in our lungs or one small drop of poison in an otherwise clean glass of water, sin has a poisonous effect on our souls.

Nobody's perfect

Years ago, comedian Jim Carrey starred in the movie *Liar, Liar* (1997), where his character (Fletcher Reede) couldn't lie for a full day. We often say that outgoing people "don't have a filter" when they talk. But imagine if this were really true. What if you couldn't hold back what you were thinking or feeling about other people—ever? Every selfish inclination, every lustful urge, every dishonest decision, every judgmental thought—all would become perfectly transparent.

How long could your friends stand to be around you? What would this do to your chances in dating or marriage? If this

happened to me, I know that I'd quickly become a very
lonely person!

But if God is really all-knowing, then he surely knows all of
our thoughts, motives, and intentions (Jer. 17:9-10; 1 Cor.
4:5). Thus it's no wonder that the Bible teaches that *all*
people are sinful—not just a select few. Throughout the
Bible, we read:

> All have sinned and fallen short of the glory of God.
> (Rom. 3:23)

> There is no man who does not sin. (1 Kings 8:46)

> There is not a righteous man on earth who
> continually does good and who never sins. (Eccl.
> 7:20)

> If You, Lord, should mark iniquities, O Lord, who
> could stand? (Ps. 130:3)

> In Your sight no man living is righteous. (Ps. 143:2)

> Who can say, 'I have cleansed my heart, I am pure
> from my sin'? (Prov. 20:9)

Surely we haven't all committed an equal number of sins or
even the same severity of sins. Yet we've all sinned to some
degree, and our good deeds can never make up for this fact.

Imagine paying for a parking ticket. The woman behind the
counter tells you, "That'll be $42 for the ticket." Now just
imagine trying to talk your way out of the ticket by telling
her, "Ma'am, before I pay for the ticket, I just want you to
know... I've never murdered anybody." What would she
say in response? She'd probably say, "That's great... Now,
the parking ticket will just be $42!"

In a similar way, God won't judge us for murder if we've never murdered anyone. But how will he hold us responsible for the ways we have hurt others?

"I don't feel guilty…"

We typically don't feel like we deserve serious consequences for our actions. That's why we don't allow accused criminals to sit on juries for their own trials. We simply can't trust them to be objective. If a judge asked the typical criminal how much time he deserved in prison, he might shrug his shoulders and say, "Mmmm… How does two days sound?"[2]

Even the worst criminals feel this way about their crimes. For instance, Adolf Eichmann—one of the chief organizers of the Nazi Holocaust—argued that he shouldn't be punished for his war crimes. He famously implored the authorities, "I was not a responsible leader, and as such do not feel myself guilty."[3] How do you think the judge received his plea? Needless to say, it didn't go well for Adolf Eichmann. It didn't matter to the court if he *felt* guilty; it mattered that he *was* guilty.

The Solution? Grace!

At this point (if you're anything like me) you might be squirming in your seat a little bit. Even *one* sin will exclude us from Heaven? If this is true, will *anybody* make it to Heaven?

---

[2] I am indebted to my friend and mentor Dennis McCallum for this helpful insight.
[3] Isabel Kershner, "Pardon Plea by Adolf Eichmann, Nazi War Criminal, Is Made Public." *The New York Times*, January 27, 2016.

Here is the good news.

We cannot earn Heaven. In fact, it would be rather odd if we could. What could you possibly do in your short time on Earth that would warrant eternity in Paradise? If a week-long trip to Hawaii costs several thousand dollars, how much will *eternity* in Heaven cost you?

The Bible teaches that Heaven comes with an infinite price tag that we could never afford. God designed Heaven so that none of us could claim that we deserved to be there. We only embarrass ourselves by trying to pay out of our small reservoir of good works.

Instead of demanding perfection, God gave us another option altogether: God wants to give eternal life to us—free of charge—through the work of Christ. Read these Scriptures for yourself:

> To the one who does not work, but believes in Him who justifies the ungodly, his faith is credited as righteousness. (Rom. 4:5)

> For by grace you have been saved through faith; and that not of yourselves, it is the gift of God; not as a result of works, so that no one may boast. (Eph. 2:8-9)

> I do not nullify the grace of God, for if righteousness comes through the Law, then Christ died needlessly. (Gal. 2:21)

As Jesus was dying, two men hung on crosses next to him "insulting Him" (Mk. 15:32). Right before his death, one of the crucified men changed his attitude. He said, "Jesus, remember me when You come in Your kingdom!" (Lk. 23:42). It might go without saying, but with his hands and feet nailed to the cross, this man could hardly perform any good works! Yet because he expressed this simple act of faith, Jesus told him, "Truly I say to you, today you shall be with Me in Paradise" (Lk. 23:43).

Hours later, one of those men went to Heaven, and the other went to Hell. It wasn't because one was "good enough" for God, and the other wasn't. It was only because one turned to Christ for forgiveness, and God gladly gave it to him.

On the Cross, Jesus exclaimed, "It is finished!" (Jn. 19:30). He completely paid for *all* of our sins: past, present, and future. After we receive Christ's forgiveness, Paul writes that God "has forgiven" us (Eph. 4:32) for "all our transgressions" (Col. 2:13). Because of Jesus' work on the Cross, Paul writes that there is "no condemnation for those who are in Christ Jesus" (Rom. 8:1).

The scandal of grace

This might sound like the best news you've ever heard. In fact, when Jesus' disciples thought up a name for this message, they called it just that: "the good news." Yet what sounds like the best news to one person, can sound wildly offensive to others.

Paul wrote that many religious people considered Jesus' death to be a "stumbling block" (1 Cor. 1:23). He used the Greek word *skandalon* here, which is the root for our English word "scandal" or "scandalous." Self-righteous people have a very difficult time accepting Jesus' forgiveness, because it seems so humbling to merely trust in Him, rather than in their good works. Many people prefer *self-righteousness,*

rather than trusting in *God's righteousness*. Jesus told a story
to illustrate this key difference:

> Two men went to the Temple to pray. One was a
> Pharisee, and the other was a despised tax collector.
> [11] The Pharisee stood by himself and prayed this
> prayer: 'I thank you, God, that I am not a sinner like
> everyone else. For I don't cheat, I don't sin, and I
> don't commit adultery. I'm certainly not like that tax
> collector! [12] I fast twice a week, and I give you a tenth
> of my income.' [13] "But the tax collector stood at a
> distance and dared not even lift his eyes to heaven as
> he prayed. Instead, he beat his chest in sorrow,
> saying, 'O God, be merciful to me, for I am a sinner.'
> [14] I tell you, this sinner, not the Pharisee, returned
> home justified before God. (Lk. 18:10-14 NLT)

This is the scandal of grace! According to Jesus, the "sinner"
finds mercy, but the self-righteous person faces judgment.

To a self-righteous person, pure and unadulterated grace
sounds "too good to be true." It sounds "too easy."
Consequently, it offends the self-righteous mindset too
much. It hurts our pride to admit that we have nothing to
offer God—nothing to force Him to accept us. Instead, we
can only open our empty hands, and accept Him and His
forgiveness. As Paul writes so simply and clearly, "If you
confess with your mouth Jesus as Lord, and believe in your
heart that God raised Him from the dead, you will be
saved" (Rom. 10:9).

Receiving the gift

Since 2008, roughly $44 billion have gone to waste in unspent gift cards, and the number rises each year.[4] Eventually, these cards are worth less than the plastic on which they're printed. Billions of dollars unspent. What a waste!

To a much greater degree, many people forfeit the gift of eternal life because they have simply never asked for it. The grace of God is not unconditional. God puts one (and only one) condition on his grace and forgiveness…

We need to *receive* it.

Scientists will never discover the "Christian gene" on the human genome. No one is born a Christian; it's something we need to choose. Some people think that they are Christians because their parents were Christians. But relationships don't work this way. If you can't remember a time that you started a relationship with a person, you probably never did. Starting a relationship with your Creator is something you tend to remember.

You can stand in a garage, but that doesn't make you a mechanic. You can stand in a kitchen, but that doesn't make you a chef. You can wear a tutu, but that doesn't make you a ballerina! In the same way, *you can stand in a church, but this doesn't make you a Christian*. If you want forgiveness, you need to ask for it. John writes, "To all who *received* him, to those who *believed* in his name, he gave the right to become children of God" (Jn. 1:12 NIV).

---

[4] Gregory Bresiger, "Unused gift cards total $44B since 2008: study." *New York Post.* January 26, 2014.

There is one thing God won't do: he won't *force* a relationship onto you. Jesus said, "I stand at the door and knock. If you hear my voice and open the door, I will come in, and we will share a meal together as friends" (Rev. 3:20). Christ will *knock* at the door of our hearts, but he won't *knock down* the door. He expects us to open the door and let Him in.

The Bible never explains what words to use to receive Christ. God doesn't want a scripted prayer or magic words. Instead, he wants a free expression of the heart, whereby you ask for a relationship with your Creator on the basis of Jesus' work on the Cross.

God doesn't want us to spend every day worried about where we'll spend eternity — wondering if our good deeds will outweigh our bad ones — worried whether we'll end up in Heaven or in Hell. Why would a loving God want us to live in such constant fear?

Far from it. As our loving father, God wants us to have security in where we're going to spend eternity. If you're ready to take Christ up on his offer, turn to him right now and receive him into your life, "so that you may know that you have eternal life" (1 Jn. 5:13).

Chapter 3: Imagine there's no Heaven

Envision waking up after a tragic plane crash. As consciousness returns, you discover that you've washed ashore on a small, mile-wide island with a couple of other survivors. No matter how many times you scour the island, you discover only enough food and water to last you another two days at most. You and the small company of survivors will soon die, and there's no stopping it. No radio. No provisions. No help. No hope.

Here's the question: Given your certain fate of death, could your time on the island be *significant* in any way?

You might spend your time drawing stick figures or playing tic-tac-toe in the sand. You might climb a palm tree, go swimming in the ocean, or work on your suntan. You might break into the flight attendants' liquor cabinet on the plane, making rum and coconut cocktails, drinking your final days away in the hot sun. *But would any of these actions or activities be meaningful?* Surely not. No matter how you change the landscape of the island or impact your fellow survivors, all of your activities would result in oblivion.

Now, what could give meaning to your time on the island?

Could a *bigger island* give meaning to your activities? Of course not. Surely it isn't the *size* of the island that's the problem. The island could be twice as big or even a hundred times bigger, but the *size* of the island wouldn't change your lack of meaning on it.

What about the *number of survivors* on the island? Would the surviving population of people change your lack of meaning? I can't see how. If two or three people lack meaning, then two or three *billion* people wouldn't bring any more. Merely adding people to the island wouldn't change the fact that death will wipe away your individual or collective footprint relatively soon.

And what about the *amount of time* you spent on the island? This wouldn't give you any more meaning than before; rather it would simply give you more time to spend on pointless activities. Whether you lived for *two* days or *two* years—nothing would change your inherent lack of purpose.

At this point, I'm sure you can see the meaning of this illustration: We *are* on the island. It's called Earth, and no one gets out alive. Our island happens to be 25,000 miles in circumference, and it has a population of seven billion. Our provisions might last for two decades or maybe two millennia. We're not sure. But we are sure of one important fact: our fate includes death.

In order to have any objective meaning, we need to survive this fate.

We need to get off the island alive.

The certainty of death

Given the reality of death, some atheistic thinkers simply bite the existential bullet and admit that there is no objective meaning to life. Author Gore Vidal once wrote, "Because there is no cosmic point to the life that each of us perceives on this distant bit of dust at galaxy's edge, all the more reason for us to maintain in proper balance what we have here. Because there is nothing else. No thing. This is it."[1] Likewise journalist James Haught writes, "We simply must try to make life as good as possible and avoid horrors and care about people and have fun, even though we know that oblivion is coming."[2] Regarding the finality of death, John Shelby Spong writes,

> Deeply loving relationships turn into aching voids. It is not being negative to say that all self-conscious life is by its very nature ultimately tragic. Mother Nature in the last analysis annihilates all of her children... This sweetness, this joy and these relationships are always lived out in the context of a trajectory that is ultimately fragile, finite and painful.[3]

In his short story "The Wall," atheist Jean-Paul Sartre explains the plight of a prisoner of war caught in a death camp. Guards tell the prisoner that they will execute him the next morning: death by firing squad against "the wall." As execution approaches, the prisoner realizes the insignificance of his life—given his certain fate in death. As he reflects on his imminent death, Sartre writes, "Several hours or several years of waiting is all the same *when you have lost the illusion of being eternal.*"[4]

---

[1] Gore Vidal, "Armageddon?" in *United States: Essays 1952-1992* (New York: Random House, 1993; Broadway Books, 2001), 1006. Cited in Hank Hanegraaff, *AfterLife: What You Really Want to Know About Heaven* (Brentwood, TN: Worthy Publishing, 2013), 70.

[2] James A. Haught, *Honest Doubt: Essays on Atheism in a Believing Society* (Amherst, NY: Prometheus, 2007), 45.

[3] John Shelby Spong, *Eternal Life: A New Vision: Beyond Religion, beyond Theism, beyond Heaven and Hell* (New York: Harper One, 2009), 116.

[4] Emphasis mine. Jean-Paul Sartre, *The Wall* (New York: New Direction Books, 1948), 12.

Under an atheistic worldview, the inevitability of death
haunts us. Anthropologist Ernest Becker writes, "The idea of
death, the fear of it, haunts the human animal like nothing
else; it is the mainspring of human activity—activity
designed largely to avoid the fatality of death, to overcome
it by denying in some way that it is the final destiny of
man."[5] As a result, Becker argues that humans strive to
"transcend death by participating in something of lasting
worth."[6] Nevertheless, in a universe without God, nothing
ultimately lasts. The question is not *whether* the labor of our
lives will crumble, but rather *when* this will occur. In an
atheistic universe, death always gets the final word.
Agnostic Bertrand Russell writes,

> All the labors of the ages, all the devotion, all the
> inspiration, all the noonday brightness of human
> genius, are destined to extinction in the vast death of
> the solar system... Man's achievement must
> inevitably be buried beneath the debris of a universe
> in ruins... How, in such an alien and inhuman
> world, can so powerless a creature as man preserve
> his aspirations untarnished?[7]

As a young man, Russell contemplated suicide as he
reflected on this grim implication: "I remained, however,
profoundly unhappy. There was a footpath leading across
fields to New Southgate, and I used to go there alone to
watch the sunset and contemplate suicide. I did not,
however, commit suicide, because I wished to know more of

---

[5] Ernest Becker, *The Denial of Death* (New York, Free Press, 1973), xvii.

[6] Quotation from Sam Keener. Cited in Ernest Becker, *The Denial of Death*, xiii.

[7] Bertrand Russell, *Why I Am Not a Christian: and Other Essays on Religion and Related Subjects* (New York: Simon & Schuster, 1967), 107.

mathematics."[8] Another author explains his lack of purpose in this way:

> Imagine a happy group of morons who are engaged in work. They are carrying bricks in an open field. As soon as they have stacked all the bricks at one end of the field, they proceed to transport them to the opposite end. This continues without stop and every day of every year they are busy doing the same thing. One day one of the morons stops long enough to ask himself what he is doing. He wonders what purpose there is in carrying the bricks. And from that instant on he is not quite as content with his occupation as he had been before. *I am the moron who wonders why he is carrying the bricks.*[9]

Is this man simply exaggerating his need for meaning? Think again. He gave his life for this belief. In fact, this excerpt comes from his suicide note. Psychologist Viktor Frankl writes, "Not a few cases of suicide can be traced back to this existential vacuum. Such widespread phenomena as depression, aggression and addiction are not understandable unless we recognize the existential vacuum underlying them."[10] As atheist Albert Camus powerfully writes, "For anyone who is alone, without God and without a master, the weight of days is dreadful."[11]

---

[8] Bertrand Russell, *The Autobiography of Bertrand Russell* (Abington: Routledge, 2009), 32.

[9] Emphasis mine. Irvin Yalom, *Existential Psychotherapy* (Basic Books, 1980), 419.

[10] Viktor E. Frankl, *Man's Search for Meaning: an Introduction to Logotherapy* (New York: Simon & Schuster, 1984), 112.

[11] Albert Camus, *The Fall* (New York: Vintage Books, 1991), 133.

During my undergraduate study, I wrote a ten-page paper for my final class. Before I could save it to my hard drive, the computer froze, erasing all of my work. A sinking feeling of frustration and remorse filled my stomach, as my forehead struck the keyboard over and over.

All of my work… gone… forever! I felt sick.

But truly, everyone who builds his or her life apart from God will have precisely the same feeling—and to an unimaginable degree. We won't lose a term paper or a letter grade; we'll lose everything.

Most people today would be able to identify LeBron James or Kobe Bryant in a photograph. But what if we showed pictures of Magic Johnson or Julius Erving? Walt Frazier (a two time NBA champion) or Bob Lanier (an eight time NBA All-Star)? Or what about Neil Johnston—an athlete who led the NBA in scoring for three consecutive seasons (1952-1954), even playing in six NBA All-Star Games? How many could recognize Neil Johnston in a photo or have even heard of him before?

Fame can give us many things, but it cannot give us meaning. Eventually, the arenas will all empty, and the newspapers or tabloids will forget all about us (if they ever noticed us at all). Whether we get "fifteen minutes of fame" or fifteen years of it, our notoriety will surely and inevitably fade.

Can't we just create our own meaning to life?

Some atheistic thinkers argue that we can create our own meaning to life, rather than seeking one from God or eternity.[12] But while we might create a *relative* or *subjective* meaning to life, we cannot produce an *objective* one. One person might find it meaningful to build a massive *Fortune 500* company, while another might find it meaningful to build a massive guild in *World of Warcraft*. If life lacks any objective meaning, then any meaning we impose upon it would be just as trivial as any other.

Surely we can still have spurts of *pleasure* in the absence of God, but we cannot have *meaning*. Often atheistic thinkers treat the terms "meaning" and "pleasure" as identical terms, but this is not always the case. *Meaning* refers to the importance or significance of our lives; it asks the question, "Why does it matter?" *Pleasure* relates to enjoyment, happiness, or sensual gratification; it asks the question, "How do I feel?" Sometimes we can experience pleasure, but lack meaning, or vice versa. Atheistic philosopher Julian Baggini notes, "In developed Western countries, we have access to more and better sources of pleasure than our predecessors could imagine. Yet we are not a noticeably fulfilled bunch."[13] Likewise, Viktor Frankl wisely observes, "People have enough to live *by* but nothing to live *for*; they have the means but no meaning."[14]

Is life meaningful because it's short?

Some atheistic thinkers argue that life is meaningful because it's short, rather than eternal. Since we have only a few short years to enjoy, we should adopt the view of *carpe diem*

---

[12] See Kai Nielsen, *Atheism and Philosophy* (New York: Prometheus, 2005), 221-222.

[13] Julian Baggini, *Atheism: A Very Short Introduction* (Oxford: Oxford UP, 2003), 67.

[14] Viktor E. Frankl, *Man's Search for Meaning*, 142.

("seize the day"), making the most of our time while it still lasts.

Yet if the shortness of life gives it meaning, then an eighty year old woman would have a less meaningful life than an eight year old girl. In fact, it would be better for children to die young in order to ensure their meaning to life!

The concept of "seizing the day" doesn't offer meaning if there is no objective meaning to seize. As atheistic philosopher Julian Baggini writes, "[*Carpe diem*] in no way provides a meaning for life. It doesn't tell us *what* to do in life, it tells us *how* to do it... As to where we find meaning, *carpe diem* is mute."[15]

Can we medicate meaning?

In his book *An Atheist's Guide to Reality* (2011), philosopher Alex Rosenberg raises the question of what we should do if we do not feel like we can live without an ultimate meaning or purpose to life. His solution?

> Take two of whatever neuro-pharmacology prescribes. If you don't feel better in the morning... or three weeks from now, switch to another one.... What should you do if you feel the tragic sense of life, if you really feel you need to find the meaning of life in order to keep living, and if you feel nothing will meet that need? Scientism tells you to treat introspection as a symptom.[16]

---

[15] Julian Baggini, *What's It All About?* 135.
[16] Alexander Rosenberg, *The Atheist's Guide to Reality: Enjoying Life without Illusions* (New York: W.W. Norton, 2011), 282-285.

This reduces our lack of meaning to something physical — like a virus or the common cold. It treats the symptoms, but not the disease, like giving morphine to a cancer patient or whiskey to a wounded soldier. While it might alleviate the pain, it doesn't fix the problem. We cannot exchange purpose for Prozac.

Machine minds and meaning

Ray Kurzweil leads the "Singularity Movement," which is a group of people who hope to scan their minds into computer brains and machine bodies.[17] Kurzweil hopes to elude death (or become cryogenically frozen) until this technology appears, allowing him to "live forever."

Yet even if this science fiction technology did exist (which it doesn't), it still wouldn't offer eternal life. Under a naturalistic worldview, we can't *transfer* ourselves into a machine body; instead, we can merely *duplicate* ourselves with it. While the duplicate machine would survive, *we* still wouldn't. Remember, within an atheistic worldview, we don't have a soul that could transfer to another body. We only have physical components that could be copied.

To see this clearly, imagine if a scientist made a perfect replica robot. After the copy was complete, would it be ethically acceptable for the scientist to incinerate your body or torture you to death? As you painfully died, would it console you to know that your android body would "live forever"? Of course not! Such a science fiction dream of eternal life would be more like a nightmare.

---

[17] Lev Grossman, "2045: The Year Man Becomes Immortal," *Time*, Thursday, Feb 10, 2011.

Death doesn't get the last word

In order to have meaning to life, we need more than
eternity; we need God. If we could live forever in a broken
and fallen world, would we even want to? Consider the
vampires in Anne Rice's popular book *Interview with the
Vampire*. After centuries of living on Earth, her immortal
monsters desired death, because the pleasures of life had
become boring and banal.

Without the infinite love and joy of God, continued
existence in a fallen world would be more like Hell than
Heaven. As humanist author Aldous Huxley once observed,
"There comes a time when one asks, even of Shakespeare,
even of Beethoven, 'Is that all there is?'"[18]

Heaven doesn't merely offer a life support system that
keeps us conscious for all eternity. It offers us God — the
greatest conceivable being. Jesus said, "This is eternal life,
that they may know You, the only true God, and Jesus
Christ whom You have sent" (Jn. 17:3). In a relationship
with Christ, we not only encounter God — the greatest
conceivable good — but we also discover eternity in which
we will enjoy him forever.

---

[18] Cited in Huston Smith, *The World's Religions: Our Great Wisdom Traditions* (San Francisco: HarperOne, 2009), 19.

Chapter 4: Is Hell divine overkill?

Halloween costumes, horror movies, or humorous episodes of *South Park* often inform our understanding of Hell. When we hear the term "Hell," our minds naturally picture horns, pitchforks, and men in red spandex suits—basically all the components of music videos from the 1980s. When others think about Hell, they imagine the clammy faces and vibrato voices of fire-and-brimstone preachers, speaking about the love of God in one breath and the terrors of Hell in the next. With such conflicting, crass, or even comical representations of Hell, it shouldn't surprise us that many have decided to give up the idea altogether.

Skeptics of the Christian faith deplore Hell. John Shelby Spong calls Hell "crude, debilitating, hostile and, finally, unbelievable."[1] Atheist Bart Ehrman calls the Christian God a "never-dying eternal divine Nazi," who tortures humans forever.[2] Atheists Christopher Hitchens[3] and Richard Dawkins[4] both rhetorically claim that the doctrine of Hell brings psychological damage to children. Bertrand Russell famously wrote, "There is one very serious defect to my mind in Christ's moral character, and that is that He believed in hell. I do not myself feel that any person who is

---

[1] John Shelby Spong, *Eternal Life*, 114.

[2] Bart D. Ehrman, *Jesus, Interrupted: Revealing the Hidden Contradictions in the Bible (and Why We Don't Know about Them)* (New York: HarperOne, 2009), 276.

[3] Christopher Hitchens, *God Is Not Great: How Religion Poisons Everything* (New York: Twelve, 2007), 220.

[4] Richard Dawkins, *The God Delusion* (Boston: Houghton Mifflin, 2006), 354-366.

really profoundly humane can believe in everlasting punishment."[5] Atheistic comedian George Carlin once joked,

> Religion has actually convinced people that there's an invisible man living in the sky who watches everything you do, every minute of every day. And the invisible man has a special list of ten things he does not want you to do. And if you do any of these ten things, he has a special place, full of fire and smoke and burning and torture and anguish, where he will send you to live and suffer and burn and choke and scream and cry forever and ever until the end of time...
>
> But He loves you.[6]

While skeptics scoff at Hell and comedians joke about it, nothing is funny about the existence of Hell. Hell will not be a place of "living easy and loving free" where "all my friends are gonna be."[7] It won't be a place where we'd rather "laugh with the sinners, than cry with the saints."[8] Hell won't be a wild party with all of our buddies. It will be a place of complete and total loss. To wake up in Hell would be a horror beyond all human expression or imagination.

It is to this unpleasant subject that we now turn.

---

[5] Bertrand Russell, *Why I Am Not a Christian*, 17.

[6] George Carlin, "Religion." *You Are All Diseased*, 1999.

[7] AC/DC, "Highway to Hell," 1979.

[8] Billy Joel, "Only the Good Die Young," 1977.

Will there be fire and brimstone in Hell?

Does Hell contain literal flames? Most theologians don't think so.[9] Instead, they believe that the fires of Hell operate as symbols for God's judgment.

But doesn't the Bible use the language of flames and fire to describe Hell?

That it does. The book of Revelation describes "fire and brimstone" in Hell (Rev. 19:20; 20:10, 14-15; 21:8), and even Jesus spoke of the "unquenchable fire" (Mk. 9:43), "fiery hell" (Mt. 5:22), "furnace of fire" (Mt. 13:42), and "eternal fire" (Mt. 18:8; 25:41). Why then would we ever interpret these passages symbolically?

Before answering this question, consider another question: do you always use the term "fire" literally? Consider just a few examples:

> When a basketball player makes multiple three-point shots in a row, we might say, "He's on *fire!*"

---

[9] For just a small sample of those who reject the notion of literal flames, see John Calvin, *Institutes of the Christian Religion*. 3.25.12. Charles Hodge, *Systematic Theology* (Oak Harbor, WA: Logos Research Systems, Inc., 1952), Vol. 3, 868. Gordon Lewis, *Integrative Theology* (Grand Rapids: Zondervan, 1994), 3:470. 474. G.K. Beale, *The Book of Revelation* (Grand Rapids, MI. William B. Eerdmans Publishing Company, 1999), 1029. Kenneth Boa and Robert Bowman, *Sense and Nonsense About Heaven and Hell* (Grand Rapids, MI: Zondervan, 2009), 118. George Ladd, *A Theology of the New Testament* (Grand Rapids, MI: William B. Eerdmans Publishing Company, 1974), 196. Bruce Milne, *The Message of Heaven and Hell* (Downers Grove, IL: InterVarsity Press, 2002) 149. Leon Morris, *Revelation: An Introduction and Commentary* (Downers Grove, IL: InterVarsity Press, 1987), 174. Robert Morey, *Death and the Afterlife* (Minneapolis, MN: Bethany House, 1984), 101. Norman L. Geisler, *Baker Encyclopedia of Christian Apologetics* (Grand Rapids, MI: Baker, 1999), 312. J.P. Moreland and Lee Strobel, *The Case for Christ: A Journalist's Personal Investigation of the Evidence for Jesus* (Grand Rapids, MI: Zondervan, 2000), 176-177.

> When a dangerous temptation intrigues us, someone
> might caution, "Don't play with *fire*..."
>
> After a spell of apathy in their marriage, a couple
> might say, "We've rekindled *the fire* in our
> relationship."

Of course, when we hear these statements, no one would
ever think of reaching for the fire extinguisher! Similarly, the
Bible uses the concept of "fire" to symbolically describe lust
(Prov. 6:27-29), unbridled anger (Hos. 7:6), uncontrolled
speech (Jas. 3:6), and even God's jealousy (Deut. 4:24). In
fact, the Scriptures describe God himself as a "consuming
fire" (Heb. 12:29). But as philosopher J.P. Moreland once
quipped, "Yet nobody thinks God is a cosmic Bunsen
burner."[10]

While the Bible refers to the "fires" of Hell, it also portrays
Hell as a "[pit] of darkness" (2 Pet. 2:4), "black darkness"
(Jude 13), or the "outer darkness" (Mt. 8:12; 22:13; 25:30).
Ask yourself: how could Hell contain *fire* and *darkness* at the
same time? Moreover, how could *physical* flames affect
spiritual beings like Satan or his angels (Mt. 25:41)?
Contradictions like these imply that we are reading these
concepts too rigidly.

So do symbolic flames and symbolic darkness let us off the
hook? Will Hell be a pretty pleasant experience after all?
Not at all. These symbols actually speak of shocking
spiritual realities that await those in Hell. If a recovering
alcoholic said that he "hit rock bottom," you wouldn't take
his statement *literally*, but you would take it *seriously*.
Likewise, the loss of eternal life will be an unspeakable

---

[10] J.P. Moreland and Lee Strobel, *The Case for Christ*, 176.

horror—a reality of judgment, grief, and irreversible alienation.

Flames symbolize how God will actively judge humanity. God promises to repay people for the ways they've morally violated others (Heb. 10:30; Rom. 12:19), and this judgment will be "according to [their] deeds" (Rom. 2:5-6). Of course, this judgment will be delivered fairly for each person. Jesus states that some people will be given *"many* lashes" (Lk. 12:47), while others "receive but *few*" (Lk. 12:47-48). He also spoke of some who will "receive *greater* condemnation" in Hell (Lk. 20:47).

Darkness depicts the passive judgment of God: loneliness and grief. For some, Jesus will say, "I never knew you; *depart from Me*" (Mt. 7:23). Paul writes, "These will pay the penalty of eternal destruction, *away from the presence of the Lord* and from the glory of His power" (2 Thess. 1:9). In a great and terrible act of fairness, God will respect our decision to reject him—forever. C.S. Lewis writes, "There are only two kinds of people in the end: those who say to God, 'Thy will be done', and those to whom God says, in the end, '*Thy* will be done.'"[11]

Jesus described Hell as a place of "weeping and gnashing of teeth" (Mt. 8:12). Does this mean that Hell will be a divine torture chamber? Not at all. Luke records the Pharisees "gnashing their teeth" at Stephen's teaching about the grace of God (Acts 7:54). Of course, this cannot refer to physical torture. Stephen was not torturing the Pharisees; in fact, the Pharisees were torturing Stephen! The Pharisees were "gnashing their teeth" because they were "resisting the Holy

---

[11] C. S. Lewis, *The Great Divorce* (New York: Macmillan, 1946), 69.

Spirit" (Acts 7:51). Philosopher Norman Geisler explains this imagery: "It is the weeping and gnashing of teeth that results from the realization that we blew it and deserve the consequences. Just as a football player may pound on the ground in agony after missing a play that loses the Super Bowl, so those in hell know that the pain they suffer is self-induced."[12]

Why is Hell eternal?

Skeptic David Mills calls the length of Hell "cruel and unusual punishment."[13] After all, why does God deliver an *eternal* judgment if we've only sinned for a *limited* amount of time?

Some philosophers and theologians resolve this issue by noting that judgment continues *eternally* because people in Hell will sin *continually*.[14] After all, John describes Hell in this way: "Let the one who does wrong, *still do wrong*; and the one who is filthy, *still be filthy*" (Rev. 22:11). If people rebelled against the love of God on Earth, how do you think they'll feel about God after he sends them to Hell?

Others note that even in our legal system, the duration of the *crime* doesn't necessarily equal the duration of the *punishment*. It might only take a minute or two to beat

---

[12] Norman L. Geisler, *If God, Why Evil?: A New Way to Think about the Question* (Minneapolis, MN: Bethany House, 2011), 104.

[13] David Mills, *Atheist Universe: the Thinking Person's Answer to Christian Fundamentalism* (Berkeley, Ca.: Ulysses, 2006), 187.

[14] Philosopher Michael Murray illustrates this principle with our legal system: A convict might initially be sentenced to prison for twenty years, but he could incur later sentencing for crimes committed while in prison. Michael J. Murray, *Reason for the Hope Within* (Grand Rapids, MI: William B. Eerdmans Publishing Company, 1999), 293.

someone to death, but the punishment shouldn't be 60 seconds long. This crime of passion would result in a life sentence.

When determining the severity of a crime, we can't just look at the moral violation; we also need to the look at the *object* of the violation. If we threaten to kill our neighbor, we might receive a restraining order. However, if we threaten to kill the President of the United States, we will receive time in a federal prison—just as stealing money from a federal bank receives a greater punishment than stealing from a gas station.

When school boys incinerate ants with magnifying glasses in the summer sun, we don't decry the horrors of "ant genocide." Why not? This activity doesn't morally offend us because of the being it violates—namely, an ant. However if young boys set fire to a *dog*, it would be a much more serious offense; and if they tortured a *human being*, the punishment would be even greater still. Of course, this ethical reasoning leads us to a very uncomfortable question: *What happens when we violate God—the greatest conceivable Being?* What should the punishment be then? Since God is the greatest conceivable being, the Bible states that morally violating him warrants an incommensurable punishment: Hell.

Have we morally violated God or just people?

My wife recently took our two-year-old son to the park down the street. As my son made his way onto the jungle gym, two seven year old boys started to tease him. How do you think my wife reacted to her son being pushed face first onto a bed of wood chips? I don't need to go into detail, but let me assure you, it wasn't pretty!

Now imagine if one of the boys told my wife, "Hey lady, we don't have a problem with *you*... We've got a problem with the *toddler*... Back off!" Would she find this argument valid? Would you? Not a chance! If someone hurts your child, it would be like hurting you. In fact, it would likely hurt more. Most parents would rather endure harm than see their children suffer.

To a far greater degree, God loves all people, and he sees the world through omniscient eyes. Every time we've victimized another person, God experiences these violations. Jesus said, "To the extent that you did it to one of these brothers of Mine, even the least of them, *you did it to Me*" (Mt. 25:40; cf. Acts 9:4; Ps. 51:4; Prov. 14:31). God isn't an emotionless and impersonal Force; he's a relational being who takes our suffering personally.

Humans are in no position to set the sentence of hell

As a high school student, I took a job bussing tables at a local Italian restaurant. It's hard to describe how my clothes would smell at the end of a shift—an interesting cocktail of grease, sweat, and spaghetti sauce. Yet after a long night at work, I could no longer smell the stench because I had been saturated in it for so long. I wouldn't dare go on a date or to a party in my work clothes. No one would stand within a ten foot radius!

In a similar way, we've always been immersed in the evil of a fallen world, and we've never known anything else. Sometimes a case of rape or murder or torture will inflame our conscience, but most often, we joke or laugh at the sin around us.

Is it any wonder why we don't understand God's judgment? We don't understand his *judgment* for sin, because we don't understand the *severity* of sin.

Why doesn't God give people a second chance after death?

The Bible doesn't teach that people will be given a second chance to find forgiveness after death. The author of Hebrews writes, "Each person is destined to die once and after that comes judgment" (Heb. 9:27 NLT). The Bible describes Hell in this way: "Between us and you there is a *great chasm fixed*, so that those who wish to come over from here to you will not be able, and that none may cross over from there to us" (Lk. 16:26). Regarding Judas, Jesus said, "It would have been good for that man if he had not been born" (Mt. 26:24). If Judas eventually chose to leave Hell, then it *would* have been good for him to be born.

But hypothetically speaking, would people choose to leave Hell if they were given the option? We might assume that they would, given the choice, but perhaps they wouldn't. Without a change of heart, Heaven would be Hell for them. Atheist Christopher Hitchens once said:

> Do I think I'm going to paradise? Of course not. I wouldn't go if I was asked. I don't want to live in some... celestial North Korea for one thing, where all

> I get to do is praise the 'Dear Leader' from dawn
> until dusk! I don't want this! It would be hell for
> me![15]

God will not take a person to Heaven against his or her will.
Of course, no one would ever *wish* to go to Hell, but they do
intentionally choose to go there. Again Geisler writes,

> Men do not *want* war, but neither do they *will* to
> eliminate what causes it. Unless we begin to will
> conditions of peace, we will continue to have war. A
> wino doesn't *want* a hangover, but he *wills* himself
> one when he drinks. So it is with hell. Those who go
> there choose the conditions but do not relish the
> consequences.[16]

After we die, we won't make a decision on whether we want
to go to Heaven or Hell; instead we will discover the
decision we've already made.

Isn't judgment unloving?

In 2014, a married woman pressed charges against her
husband for drugging and raping her. She suspected that
her husband had been abusing her for over three years, so
she recorded the crime and subsequently pressed charges.
But while the video evidence clearly convicted her husband,
the Indiana judge didn't sentence the man to any kind of
punishment. In fact, the judge told her at the sentencing that
she "needed to forgive her attacker."

---

[15] Christopher Hitchens, Peter Gomes, Harold Kushner. The Connecticut Forum.
"God: Big Questions, Bigger Questions." January 29, 2009.
[16] Norman L. Geisler, *The Roots of Evil* (Grand Rapids, MI: Zondervan Pub. House,
1978), 88.

After the hearing, the abused woman stated, "I was very pleased with the *conviction*, but the *sentencing* was a bit of a punch to the gut by the justice system."[17] Of course, the public nearly called for the judge's head on a platter! Comments about the case abounded: "You are a *disgrace* to your profession... You should be *ashamed* of yourself for your *ridiculous* sentence... I will do *everything in my power* to make sure you are *NOT re-elected* in November."

Could you imagine meeting this judge after the court case had adjourned? Would you shake his hand? Would you be able to look him in the eye? Of course not. You wouldn't *talk* to that judge; you wouldn't *respect* that judge; most importantly, you wouldn't *love* that judge.

The same is true for God. If God didn't judge evil, he wouldn't be loving. Holocaust survivor Elie Wiesel famously wrote, "The opposite of love is not hate, it's indifference."[18] We could never love a God who looks at evil and suffering with indifference. A being like that wouldn't be worthy of love or respect. This is the great irony of denying Hell: It doesn't make God more loving, but less. If God ignored evil, then he would become evil in the process.

We often decry the problem of evil in the world, but then we turn around and criticize the solution to evil: judgment. But we can't have it both ways. God's answer for the problem of evil is judgment. To be sure, the thought of Hell weighs heavily on our hearts, but so does our world filled with evil and suffering. We witness millions dying from hunger,

[17] Emphasis mine. Matt Pearce, "Indiana judge assailed for light sentence in husband-wife rape case." *Los Angeles Times.* May 20, 2014.
[18] U.S. News and World Report. 27. October, 1986. Cited in Elizabeth Knowles, *The Oxford Dictionary of Quotations* (Oxford: Oxford University Press, 2001), 816.

while millions of others die of obesity. We see holocausts, genocide, and warfare—racism, torture, and death. While judgment doesn't always make sense, neither does our world filled with pain and horror.

Many people want to do away with Hell, thinking that God will just forgive us or perhaps ignore how we have hurt others. But ask yourself: If this happens, what did it cost God to forgive my sins?[19] If God just "looked the other way," then all of the pain, all of the suffering, all of the evil in the world—it cost God nothing to remedy it.

Under the biblical view, forgiveness cost God *everything*. It cost him the death of his Son. As Jesus hung from the Cross, he cried, "My God, My God, why have You forsaken Me?" (Mt. 27:46) Jesus suffered the pain of Hell—separation and judgment from the Father—so we would never need to know what this is like. In the end, the same God who sentences people to Hell is the same God who suffered Hell to reach us.

Why does Hell bother us so much?

If you're still feeling disturbed by the biblical teaching on Hell, I don't blame you. It bothers me quite a bit. In fact, if this biblical teaching doesn't bother you, I think something might be drastically wrong.

Consider God's words in Ezekiel: "As surely as I live, says the Sovereign Lord, I take no pleasure in the death of wicked people. I only want them to turn from their wicked ways so they can live. Turn! Turn from your wickedness, O

---

[19] Timothy Keller (ed. Christopher Morgan & Robert Peterson), *Is Hell for Real or Does Everyone Go to Heaven?* (Grand Rapids, MI: Zondervan, 2011), 78.

people of Israel! Why should you die? (Ezek. 33:11 NLT)." Or reflect on the words of the prophet Jeremiah: "[God] does not willingly bring affliction or grief to any human being" (Lam. 3:33 TNIV). Here, we see the very heart of God in regards to people who reject him. Will God judge these people? *Yes.* Will he enjoy judgment? *Not at all!*

We find the same teaching in the New Testament. Peter writes, "[God] is patient toward you, not wishing for *any* to perish but for *all* to come to repentance" (2 Pet. 3:9; cf. 1 Tim. 2:3-4). Jesus himself taught, "It is not the will of your Father who is in heaven that one of these little ones perish" (Mt. 18:14).

Do you see why Hell bothers our conscience so much, and why it is only natural that we would feel so disturbed at the thought of someone going to Hell?

It bothers *us*, because it bothers *God*.

The stakes are high

When we hear bad news, we often react with denial. According to a recent poll, 76% of Americans believe in Hell, yet only one-half of one percent believe that they will go there.[20] But denial doesn't change reality. If Hell exists, our opinions about it don't make the slightest difference.

According to Jesus Christ, Hell is a tragic reality. The most loving, caring, and compassionate man who ever walked the face of the Earth taught about Hell in the starkest of terms (Mt. 5:22; 5:29-30; 10:28; 13:49-50; 18:8-9; 23:15; 33; 25:46; Mk. 9:43; Lk. 16:19-31). In fact, Jesus spoke about Hell

---

[20] Barna Group. "Americans Describe Their Views About Life After Death." October 21, 2003.

in the most terrifying and vivid language imaginable, so that no one would ever decide to go there.

As we conclude, ask yourself: Wouldn't it be just horrible if you read through this entire chapter on Hell, and you ended up going there?

There's good news: you never need to know what Hell will be like. Jesus said, "I tell you the truth, those who listen to my message and believe in God who sent me have eternal life. They will never be condemned for their sins, but they have already passed from death into life" (Jn. 5:24 NLT).

Chapter 5: A sneak preview of eternal life

Every so often, movie trailers appear on YouTube to promote the best blockbusters Hollywood has to offer. Even though these trailers don't show the entirety of the film, they give just enough to whet the appetite. After watching a tantalizing trailer, you can't wait to see the film.

The Bible offers something similar with regard to Heaven. It provides little glimpses or snapshots that explain enough to excite us without explaining too much to ruin all of the surprises. God gives us a "sneak peek" into Heaven to mesmerize our minds and stir our souls. Let's explore these together.

A restored universe (Rev. 21:1)

> Then I saw a new heaven and a new earth; for the first heaven and the first earth passed away. (Rev. 21:1)

Hallmark greeting cards typically depict the afterlife as plump people wrapped in adult diapers, floating on the clouds in a ghost-like existence, playing harps for all of eternity. But such a distorted picture more adequately describes Hell than Heaven.

According to the Bible, we will not ultimately escape Earth to go to Heaven, but rather, Heaven will invade and take over the Earth. The Bible describes Heaven as an entirely restored universe—not some ethereal existence in the clouds. John writes, "I saw a new heaven and a new earth" (Rev. 21:1), which is a compound phrase describing a new physical universe (cf. Gen. 1:1).[1]

Some theologians believe that our world will be *replaced*, rather than *restored*.[2] From this viewpoint, God will annihilate our universe and create a new one from scratch.[3]

Others, like myself, believe God will *renew* our world—not *replace* it.[4] If John meant to say that the "new earth" was a replacement of the old earth, he would've used the Greek word *neos*, which means "what was not there before... what

---

[1] OT scholar Bruce Waltke writes, "This *merism* represents the cosmos, meaning the organized universe in which humankind lives. In all its uses in the Old Testament..., this phrase functions as a compound referring to the organized universe." Bruce K. Waltke, *Genesis: A Commentary* (Zondervan: Grand Rapids, MI, 2001), 59.

[2] See Mark Hitchcock, *The End: A Complete Overview of Bible Prophecy and the End of Days* (Carol Stream, IL: Tyndale House, 2012), 450. Robert L. Thomas, *Revelation 8-22: An Exegetical Commentary* (Chicago: Moody, 1995), 439-440. G.R. Beasley-Murray, *Revelation* (Grand Rapids, MI: William B. Eerdmans Publishing Company, 1974), 306-307. John Walvoord, *The Revelation of Jesus Christ* (Chicago, IL: JFW Publishing Trust, 1966), 306. William R. Newell, *Revelation: A Complete Commentary* (Grand Rapids, MI: Baker Book House, 1935), 335-338.

[3] Peter writes, "The elements will be destroyed with intense heat, and the earth and its works will be burned up" (2 Pet. 3:10). Does this mean that the world will be annihilated, and then recreated from scratch? I don't think so. Earlier in this same chapter, Peter writes that God "destroyed" the world before "being flooded with water" (2 Pet. 3:6). After the Flood of Noah, was the world annihilated? Not at all. The world still existed even if God "destroyed" the surface of the Earth through the Flood. Moreover, the expression "burned up" can also be rendered "laid bare" (NET) or "exposed" (ESV). The NET note for 2 Peter 3:10 describes this as "one of the most difficult textual problems in the NT." Therefore, we would be wise not to hang too much theological significance on this one passage of Scripture.

[4] See Randy C. Alcorn, *Heaven* (Wheaton, IL: Tyndale House, 2004), 147-151. Walter Kaiser, *Preaching and Teaching the Last Things* (Grand Rapids, MI: Baker Academic, 2011), 157. Joni Eareckson Tada, *Heaven: Your Real Home* (Grand Rapids, MI: Zondervan, 1997), 68.

has only just arisen or appeared… new in time or origin."[5] But John didn't use this word. Instead, he used the word *kainos*, which means, "what is new in nature, different from the usual, impressive, better than the old, superior in value or attraction."[6] In other words, a better translation for "a *new* earth" might actually be "a *renewed* earth."

Paul uses this same term (*kainos*) to refer to how Christians become a "new creation" (2 Cor. 5:17). Just as believers in Christ will be renewed in their resurrected bodies, the entire material universe will be renewed as well. As Paul writes, "The creation itself will be liberated from its bondage to decay" (Rom. 8:21). Paul believed that the Earth would be *liberated*—not *annihilated*—in the end. After all, God promised to keep his creation "forever and ever" (Ps. 148:6).

Jesus spoke of the "regeneration" (*paliggenesia*) of the Earth (Mt. 19:28), and Paul uses this same term to explain how Christians have experienced "regeneration" at conversion (Titus 3:5). Ancient Greek philosophers used this term (*paliggensia*) to refer to the rejuvenation of the Earth. But as Colin Brown notes, "The cosmos did not attain to a new mode of being or quality through the rebirth; the world that has passed away was there once again."[7] Of course, while Greek thinkers held to a repeated destruction and renewal of the Earth, Jesus spoke of one—and only one—restoration ("*the* regeneration").

Based on the Bible's teaching then, Heaven will be a place familiar to us: oceans, mountains, trees, and sunsets. God

---

[5] Gerhard Kittel, *Theological Dictionary of the New Testament*, 3.447.

[6] Gerhard Kittel, *Theological Dictionary of the New Testament*, 3.447.

[7] J. Guhrt, *New International Dictionary of New Testament Theology* (Grand Rapids, MI: Zondervan Publishing House, 1986), 184.

will destroy the surface of the Earth in judgment, which will no doubt include our houses, cities, and architecture. But will the *continents* shift drastically? Will we be able to recognize the same mountains or beaches, and perhaps return to them? How much will remain for us to rediscover and recognize?

Some theologians even speculate that there will be space travel in Heaven.[8] After all, if we can achieve space travel today under the curse of a fallen world, why wouldn't we have it in Heaven *without* the curse? Will we spend eons discovering the enormity and grandeur of God's universe?

A restored body (1 Cor. 15:52-54; 1 Jn. 3:2)

> The dead will be raised imperishable, and we will be changed. [53] For this perishable must put on the imperishable, and this mortal must put on immortality. [54] But when this perishable will have put on the imperishable, and this mortal will have put on immortality, then will come about the saying that is written, 'Death is swallowed up in victory.' (1 Cor. 15:52-54)

> We know that when He appears, we will be like Him, because we will see Him just as He is. (1 Jn. 3:2)

> We ourselves groan within ourselves, waiting eagerly for our adoption as sons, the redemption of our body. (Rom. 8:23)

---

[8] Randy C. Alcorn, *Heaven*, 253-256.

The Bible pictures our bodies as *temporary tents*—not *permanent homes* (2 Cor. 5:1-5). When you first leave home to camp in tents, you enjoy the taste of charred hotdogs, and the smell of the great outdoors. The novelty of sleeping on an air mattress feels refreshing—for a night or two. But after a week of bug bites and using the woods as a toilet, you begin to long for home. If anything, tent camping makes you appreciate the comforts of a warm bed and a hot shower.[9]

Our lives are this way now. We can survive in these temporary tents, but when we're spiritually sober, we long for resurrected bodies. As our bodies ache from age or suffer from sickness, like Paul we can say, "We ourselves groan within ourselves, waiting eagerly for... the redemption of our body" (Rom. 8:23).

We won't be ghosts in Heaven, but glorified people with supernatural bodies.[10] Jesus rose physically from the dead, and the Bible calls Jesus a man—not a ghost (Acts 17:31; 1 Cor. 15:47; 1 Tim. 2:5). After he rose from the dead, Jesus gnawed on a piece of broiled fish (Lk. 24:42-43), and the disciples "ate and drank" with him (Acts 10:41). Christ invited the disciples to touch his physical body. He said, "See My hands and My feet, that it is I Myself; touch Me and see, *for a spirit does not have flesh and bones* as you see that I

---

[9] I am indebted to Paul Tripp for this illustration. Paul David Tripp, *Forever: Why You Can't Live Without It* (Grand Rapids, MI: Zondervan, 2011), 37-38.

[10] Some critical theologians argue that Paul calls our resurrected bodies "spiritual," rather than "natural" (1 Cor. 15:44, 46), implying a ghost-like state for our resurrected bodies. However the Greek term *pneumatikon* ("spiritual") refers to a person's spiritual orientation—not their spiritual bodies. Paul uses this same term to refer to "spiritual" people on Earth (1 Cor. 2:15; Gal. 6:1) or the "spiritual" food and water during the Exodus (1 Cor. 10:4). Of course, Paul does not mean that these were ghosts or invisible drinks! He means that these physical people and things had a spiritual orientation.

have" (Lk. 24:39). Jesus even encouraged the skeptic Thomas to feel the gory wounds in his hands and side (Jn. 20:27; cf. 1 Jn. 1:1).

It's important to take note of Jesus' resurrected body, because the Bible teaches that *we will be raised just as Jesus was raised*. John writes, "We know that when He appears, *we will be like Him*" (1 Jn. 3:2). Paul writes that Christ "will transform the body of our humble state into conformity with the body of His glory" (Phil. 3:21), and we will "bear the likeness of the man from heaven" (1 Cor. 15:49 NIV).

Jesus didn't *lose* any aspects of his earthly body, but he surely *gained* some abilities that he didn't have before. John records, "When the doors were shut where the disciples were… Jesus came and stood in their midst" (Jn. 20:19). Interpreters disagree on whether this means that Jesus *transported* through the closed doors,[11] or perhaps he simply *walked* through them.[12] Either way, Jesus had a supernatural ability to enter into a locked room. If we will be raised like Jesus, will we be able to supernaturally transport or perhaps walk through walls?

If caterpillars could reflect on life inside of their cocoon, they probably wouldn't be able to imagine bursting free as a butterfly.[13] Similarly, while we currently ache in our mortal bodies, we will be changed at the return of Christ. Paul

---

[11] For instance, Boa and Bowman write, "The common assertion that Jesus 'walked through walls' is incorrect; the texts state that he suddenly appeared in or disappeared from the room, not that he walked through a wall." Kenneth Boa and Robert Bowman, *Sense and Nonsense About Heaven and Hell*, 69.

[12] Carson writes, "As his resurrection body passed through the grave-clothes (v. 6–8), so it passed through the locked doors and simply 'materialized.'" D. A. Carson, *The Gospel According to John* (Grand Rapids, MI: Inter-Varsity Press, 1991), 646.

[13] Hank Hanegraaff, *AfterLife*, 3.

writes, "Our bodies are buried in brokenness, but they will be raised in glory. They are buried in weakness, but they will be raised in strength… We who are living will also be transformed… Our mortal bodies must be transformed into immortal bodies" (1 Cor. 15:43, 52-53 NLT). Will we be able to run marathons without gasping for air, or fall off a cliff without having a single scratch? The possibilities spark our imagination to even consider.

All of this means that we will be able to identify one another in Heaven. After all, the disciples could still "recognize" Jesus after his resurrection (Lk. 24:31), and Paul said he would be able to identify his Christian friends in Heaven (1 Thess. 2:19; cf. Mt. 8:11). In eternity, we will enjoy our time reconnecting with lost family and friends, meeting believers that impacted us whom we've never met. (Personally, I plan to open an Irish pub so I can coax C.S. Lewis into talking to me for a couple of centuries—or until he gets bored with me.)

On the final days of a good vacation, we often lament having to go back home: if only we had more time to enjoy the company of friends and family. But in Heaven, we will have eternity to enjoy one another. Joni Eareckson Tada writes, "Friendship initiated on earth barely has time to get started; we only scratch its surface in the few short years we reside on earth. Its greater and richer dimension will unfold in heaven."[14]

The best parties aren't primarily about the *place*, but about the *people* invited. If you have the right mix of people together, you can make any place enjoyable. In Heaven,

---

[14] Joni Eareckson Tada, *Heaven*, 49.

we'll spend our time in a remarkable place with remarkable people—free from sin, sickness, or selfishness.

A city (Rev. 21:2)

> I saw the holy city, new Jerusalem, coming down out of heaven from God. (Rev. 21:2)

As John wrote these words, the city of Jerusalem lay in smoldering ruins from the war with Rome. Here he sees a new city descending from Heaven—a New Jerusalem.

Theologians debate whether to take the New Jerusalem as literal or symbolic. Those who hold to a literal view[15] note that John uses the word "city" fifteen times in Revelation 21 and 22. He doesn't say it is *like* a city or as a city (using the device of simile). Instead he says it *is* a city. (Compare this with being made ready *"as a bride"* in verse 2). Furthermore, John mentions very specific architectural measurements (Rev. 21:15-17) and details about the foundation stones (Rev. 21:12-14), gates (Rev. 22:14), and building materials (Rev. 21:18-21). He tells us that the measurements correspond to those used by humans (Rev. 21:17). If the city is symbolic, why all of the detail?[16]

If we interpret the New Jerusalem to be literal, the ground floor will be 1,960,000 square miles. If it had 24 foot ceilings on each floor, it would contain 300,000 stories. This means

---

[15] Robert L. Thomas, *Revelation 8-22*, 461. John Walvoord, *The Revelation of Jesus Christ*, 321. William R. Newell, *Revelation*, 348-52.

[16] The author of Hebrews anticipates a heavenly city as well. He writes, "[Abraham] was looking for the city which has foundations, whose architect and builder is God" (Heb. 11:10), and he writes, "We are seeking the city which is to come" (Heb. 11:10; Heb. 13:14). Moreover, Paul writes that believers belong to "the Jerusalem above" (Gal. 4:26). However, theologians also dispute whether to understand these references as literal or symbolic.

that 588 billion people could each have a full square mile of real estate. Thus when Jesus told his disciples that in his Father's house there were "many dwelling places," this was a massive understatement! (Jn. 14:2)

Other interpreters believe that we're reading this section too literally. For one, the enormity of the pearls at the gates seem to speak against a literal interpretation (Rev. 21:21). How big would the oysters need to be to produce pearls of this size? The New Jerusalem also has the dimensions of a perfect cube (Rev. 21:16). Scripture mentions only one other perfect cube: the Holy of Holies in the center of the Tabernacle (1 Kings 6:19-20). Since the high priest entered this perfect cube to meet with God, these interpreters maintain that the New Jerusalem serves as a symbol for being in God's presence forever (Rev. 21:3),[17] because believers will replace the Temple of God (Rev. 13:6).[18]

Wherever we land in this debate, we shouldn't miss the forest for the trees. John describes Heaven as a city to communicate the fact that diversity and culture will fill the next life.

Cities contain diversity, trade, commerce, artistic endeavors, eclectic cuisine, education, and sporting events. Outside of the New Jerusalem, we will discover "nations" that are ruled by "kings" (Rev. 21:22-26; cf. Lk. 19:17), implying

---

[17] G.R. Beasley-Murray, *Revelation*, 322.

[18] Since the description of the New Jerusalem only occurs in *one* passage, not much is at stake in our interpretation. While it's important to hold to our interpretive convictions in other areas of eschatology (like the Millennial Kingdom which receives many biblical descriptions), we shouldn't be too dogmatic in our view of these descriptions of the New Jerusalem.

further diversity and culture from "every nation and all tribes and peoples and tongues" (Rev. 7:9).

The author of Hebrews writes that Christians "desire a better country, that is, a heavenly one" (Heb. 11:16; cf. v.14). Heaven will surely be a fusion of cultures, but we will all find unity under God. No more racism. No more wars or genocides. Humanity will finally learn to embrace its differences.

Peter describes Christians as "aliens and strangers" in the world (1 Pet. 2:11). The term "alien" means "one who lives in a place that is not one's home." Since our home is in Heaven, we are strangers in this world. Paul writes that "our citizenship is in Heaven" (Phil. 3:20). While we currently live in a foreign land, we shouldn't confuse this with our final destination. We're passing through this world until we get home.

Finally, John writes that the "gates will never be closed" (Rev. 21:25). While modern cities don't have walls, ancient cities "needed walls to protect them against the assaults of their enemies."[19] In ancient times, cities would close their gates at night to defend against enemies "breaking through [their] walls" (Ps. 144:14). In Heaven, there will be no reason to lock the doors (Isa. 60:11-12).

A marriage (Rev. 21:2)

> I saw the holy city… made ready as a bride adorned for her husband. (Rev. 21:2)

---

[19] George Ladd, *A Commentary on the Revelation of John* (Grand Rapids, MI: William B. Eerdmans Publishing Company, 1972), 282.

God uses marriage as an illustration of Jesus' love for us. John calls believers the "bride" of Christ (Rev. 21:2, 9; 22:17; cf. Isa. 61:10). Paul tells husbands to love their wives "just as Christ also loved the church and gave Himself up for her" (Eph. 5:25; cf. 5:32), and he calls the intermittent period between his ascension and return as our engagement or "betrothal" to Christ (2 Cor. 11:2).

Weddings take so long to prepare. My wife and I had a short engagement and a cheap wedding, but even then, plans and preparation dominated the months before the wedding day. To a far greater degree, Christ began preparing his wedding day with us "before the creation of the world" (Eph. 1:4). Just as couples pour time and money into their wedding, Christ footed the bill with a far greater commodity—his own blood (1 Pet. 1:19). You may have been to some pretty expensive weddings before, but nothing like this.

When my wife walked down the aisle, she looked magnificent. Her friends had prepared her hair, makeup, and dress for that one short ceremony. She looked so beautiful and breathtaking that if I was a lesser man, I might have cried. But I'm not, so I didn't. (Okay, I may have teared up a little…).

Have you ever seen an ugly bride at a wedding? That's a trick question: *There's no such thing.* Twenty four hours before the wedding, the bride might look like any other girl. But when the wedding day comes, she's stunning as she walks down the aisle. When we stand before Christ on this day, we will be completely covered by his grace and forgiveness "without stain or wrinkle or any other blemish, but holy and blameless" (Eph. 5:27 NIV).

Sadly, not everyone will be at this wedding. Just like regular weddings, Jesus' ceremony will have a guest list. Jesus told the story of a great King who threw a wedding party for his son. At the reception, the King discovered a "wedding crasher" in the room, so he asked him, "Friend, how did you get in here without wedding clothes?" But Jesus tells us that "the man was speechless" (Mt. 22:12 NIV). He had snuck in. He wasn't on the list. So the King threw him out onto the street.

Many self-righteous people currently expect to go to Heaven. Yet Christ will not tolerate self-righteousness here. Instead, he will say, "I never knew you; depart from Me, you who practice lawlessness" (Mt. 7:23). Imagine spending your entire life going to church, giving money, and saying your prayers each night. Yet because you trusted in your own righteousness to get into Heaven, you wound up going to Hell instead. What a great and terrible tragedy! If they would only turn to Christ for his righteousness, they could be part of the wedding ceremony. But sadly, many will be excluded from this fantastic moment in history.

A family (Rev. 21:7)

> I will be his God and he will be My son. (Rev. 21:7)

After my wife gave birth to our son, my life suddenly changed. A faint smell of dirty diapers began to follow me throughout each and every room of my house. Within the first few months, I had more bodily fluids spit, sprinkled, and smeared on me than I thought possible. Mysterious milky-white vomit stains began to appear all over my carpets, clothes, and furniture. High-pitched screams echoed down hallways at all hours of the night—like a broken alarm clock that only sounded whenever I began to drift to sleep. Overnight, my son developed a supernatural ability to break, chew, or hide every valuable object in my house. (In fact, I'm *still* looking for my remote control, which disappeared months ago!)

Under these conditions, you might wonder why we decided to have a child at all. But if you're a parent, you already know the answer to that question: We love our son, and no amount of screams, spills, or stains will ever change that. When he first uttered the two syllables "Da-da," my life changed forever. I developed a capacity to experience emotions that I never knew I had. With this in mind, it might shock some to discover that God calls us his sons and daughters.[20]

Many have difficulty grasping this profound biblical truth, because we grew up in such dysfunctional families or even broken homes. To some, the holidays weren't a time of rest and relaxation; these were times of anxiety or anger. For many, their fathers weren't a source of strength, wisdom, and tenderness in the home; instead their fathers were absentee or even abusive. As a result, many find it difficult to connect with the idea that God wants them to be a part of his family. It just seems too risky to open their hearts to the love of God, because they fear the disappointment it could bring. Yet they yearn for more.

---

[20] Many passages describe this great biblical truth (Rom. 8:15; 2 Cor. 6:18; Gal. 4:5-6; Heb. 12:5; Mt. 23:8; Mk. 3:32-33; 10:28-30; Gal. 6:10).

If you didn't grow up in a loving family, I'm betting you can imagine what one might look like if it could exist, and you've even *longed* for such a family. Heaven isn't just a celestial house—but a home—a place of security and tenderness.

God wants to give us the family we never had, and perhaps, can only imagine. But we need to surrender the independence of adulthood in approaching God, and instead take the humble position of being his child. Jesus said, "Whoever does not receive the kingdom of God like a child will not enter it at all" (Lk. 18:17).

Of course, Jesus doesn't want us to have a child's *gullibility* or *immaturity*, but a child's *humility* (Eph. 4:14; Mt. 10:16). Just study little children around you: they seem to enjoy the world in a way we can't anymore. When my son shouts for joy at the arrival of friends or laughs with his mother on the living room floor, I wish I could enjoy anything that much. Little children have an ability to see the world with a certain innocence and purity that we've traded for a "grown-up" cynicism or apathy.

But there's good news: we're going to regain all of the child-like wonder that we've lost. In Heaven, we'll be like the child who follows around his Father, asking, "What dat?" to all of the new and exciting features of the world around them. Finally, on this great day, we'll be "at home with the Lord" (2 Cor. 5:8).

The Bible doesn't tell us everything about Heaven. Surely there will be much to explore when we get there. But like a little kid falling asleep on Christmas Eve, the more we reflect and pray about these images of Heaven, the more anticipation we will have to go there.

Chapter 6: We won't have everything in Heaven

You might discover an apartment with cheap rent, large rooms, and a nice view. But before you sign a lease, you would also want to know that it does *not* have thin walls and loud neighbors. When we consider the reality of Heaven, the Bible doesn't just tell us what *will* be there, but what *won't* be there as well.

What can we expect to never see when we get to Heaven?

No sea (Rev. 21:1)

> There is no longer any sea. (Rev. 21:1)

No sea? This passage is very disappointing if you're a fisherman or a jet skier (or a pirate). Why would God take away the oceans and rivers, when these are some of the most beautiful portions of his creation?

But not so fast. John cannot mean that *bodies of water* will no longer exist in eternity. Just a chapter later, he mentions a river pouring through the city of Jerusalem (Rev. 22:1). We must be reading his descriptions too literally.

Revelation 17:15 informs us that the "waters" symbolize "peoples and multitudes and nations and tongues." This is why the Antichrist arises "out of the sea" (Rev. 13:1). John doesn't mean that the Antichrist is a partially aquatic man with gills and flippers! Rather, the "sea" refers to humanity in rebellion against God (cf. Dan. 7:3; Isa. 17:12). In eternity, humans will never rebel against him ever again.

Ancient people probably understood this symbolism much better than we do today. The oceans were a place of dread, danger, and death—not a place where they went snorkeling or sun tanning.[1] The "calm after the storm" wasn't just a pleasant expression to an ancient person, but a reassuring reality. The lack of the sea symbolically describes the peace of a restored creation (cf. Isa. 57:20-21).

No temple (Rev. 21:3, 22; 22:4)

> The tabernacle of God is among men, and He will dwell among them, and they shall be His people, and God Himself will be among them. (Rev. 21:3)

> I saw no temple in it, for the Lord God the Almighty and the Lamb are its temple. (Rev. 21:22)

Most religions teach that humans need temples to connect with the spiritual realm. Temples serve as a sort of crossroads between the natural and supernatural worlds, where the physical and spiritual intersect.

God instructed the ancient Jewish people to create a portable temple—called a tabernacle—to connect with him. The people of Israel couldn't just waltz into the presence of God. To see God directly would be too overwhelming—like looking at the sun without a welding mask. When Moses asked to see God directly, we read, "No man can see Me and live!" (Ex. 33:20) In fact, Moses' face glowed from even being *near* the presence of God (Ex. 34:29).

---

[1] George Ladd, *A Commentary on the Revelation of John*, 276.

With this in mind, Jesus certainly made an astonishing assertion: he claimed that his body was the Temple (Jn. 2:21). Instead of coming to God through a building or a holy place, Jesus taught that we could come to God *directly through him*. Thus when we read that there will be "no temple" in Heaven, this is because we will have uninterrupted access to God's presence through Jesus' work on the Cross. In Heaven, we won't need a temple anymore, because we "will see His face" (Rev. 22:4).

What will it be like to have direct and unconstrained access to God?

During the Vietnam War, enemy leaders held American POWs in a torture facility notoriously called the "Hanoi Hilton" in North Vietnam. The torturers isolated the men in cells, but the POWs learned to communicate to one another through Morse code. After torture sessions, the men would tap on the pipes to each another, sharing jokes, life stories, and words of encouragement. They did this for years on end until finally, the war was over, and they were rescued. After communicating for years through the rusty pipes of the prison, these men finally met each other face to face.

In a similar way, we currently have broken communication with God in a painful and fractured world. Yes, we can communicate to God through prayer and reading his words in the Bible—yet we long to meet *Him*. We've been like those men in the prison cells, tapping messages back and forth. But someday, the cells will be opened, and we'll see our Creator face to face. Paul writes, "Now we see in a mirror dimly, but then face to face; now I know in part, but

then I will know fully just as I also have been fully known"
(1 Cor. 13:12).

No death, sorrow, crying, or pain (Rev. 21:4)

> He will wipe away every tear from their eyes; and
> there will no longer be any death; there will no
> longer be any mourning, or crying, or pain; the first
> things have passed away. (Rev. 21:4)

Apparently upon arriving in Heaven, some people will still
be weeping—perhaps processing the pain from their time
on Earth. If I was God and had just brought people into
Paradise, I would probably be offended that anyone could
or would cry. I'd probably scream and yell and stomp my
feet, "There's no crying here! Suck it up and get over it!
You're in Heaven!"

Fortunately, the God of the Bible is nothing like me! Amidst
all of the love and celebration of Heaven, God will
personally stoop down and "wipe away every tear" from
our eyes (Rev. 21:4). After this, pain and suffering will cease.
For two millennia, Christians have prayed that God's will
would be done on Earth, just as it is in Heaven (Mt. 6:10). In
this day, that prayer will finally be answered.

No hunger, thirst, or heat (Rev. 7:16)

> They will hunger no longer, nor thirst anymore; nor
> will the sun beat down on them, nor any heat. (Rev.
> 7:16)

All of us hunger for Heaven metaphorically, but some
hunger for it literally. Our Christian brothers and sisters in

the third world understand this passage of Scripture in a way that we simply can't grasp.

Last year, Americans spent roughly 60 billion dollars on their pets,[2] while roughly 750 million people went to sleep malnourished worldwide.[3] Americans annually guzzle down roughly twelve billion dollars in bottled water, while most other nations don't even have access to clean water from a tap.[4] How strange it feels to walk down one hundred foot aisles of pet food in a supermarket, while millions starve across the globe.

As a dog owner and an Aquafina drinker, I don't mean any of this to inspire guilt in the reader. But can we simply agree that something is fundamentally broken in the world around us? Jesus promised that he will fix our world of poverty and hunger in Heaven. He said, "Blessed are you who hunger now, for you shall be satisfied" (Lk. 6:21).

No sun or moon (Rev. 7:16; 21:23; 22:5)

> The city has no need of the sun or of the moon to shine on it, for the glory of God has illumined it, and its lamp is the Lamb. (Rev. 21:23)

> There will no longer be any night; and they will not have need of the light of a lamp nor the light of the

---

[2] Michelle Castillo, "Americans Will Spend More Than $60 Billion on Their Pets This Year," *NBC News*, July 15, 2015.
http://www.nbcnews.com/business/consumer/americans-will-spend-more-60-billion-their-pets-year-n390181

[3] Food and Agriculture Organization of the United Nations (FAO). 2015.
http://www.fao.org/3/a-i4646e.pdf

[4] *International Bottled Water Association*, April 25, 2013.

> sun, because the Lord God will illumine them; and
> they will reign forever and ever. (Rev. 22:5)

Some Christians understand these verses to mean that we won't have a sun or moon in Heaven.[5] But look closer at the language. John doesn't state that God will annihilate the sun or moon in Heaven. Instead, he writes that we will have "no need" for them (cf. Isa. 60:19-20). Jesus claimed to be "the light of the world" (Jn. 8:12), and in Heaven, he will shine brighter than the sun (cf. Mt. 17:2).

Before the invention of the light bulb, people feared travelling at night—being utterly dependent on the light of the sun or the moon. In Heaven, we will never walk in the fear of darkness again.

No abominations (Rev. 21:27)

> Nothing unclean, and no one who practices
> abomination and lying, shall ever come into it, but
> only those whose names are written in the Lamb's
> book of life. (Rev. 21:27)

> The cowardly and unbelieving and abominable and
> murderers and immoral persons and sorcerers and
> idolaters and all liars, their part will be in the lake
> that burns with fire and brimstone, which is the
> second death. (Rev. 21:8)

> Outside are the dogs and the sorcerers and the
> immoral persons and the murderers and the
> idolaters, and everyone who loves and practices
> lying. (Rev. 22:15)

---

[5] Robert L. Thomas, *Revelation 8-22*, 475. Billy Graham, *The Heaven Answer Book* (Nashville, TN: Thomas Nelson, 2012), 59-60. Joni Eareckson Tada, *Heaven*, 27.

Regrettably, too many preachers have used these passages to teach that Heaven is only for righteous people. But this is mistaken for a number of reasons.

For one, if we use these passages to threaten someone's relationship with God, then we should use them consistently. Which one of us has never lied? Never been cowardly? Never been unbelieving? If we take this passage literally, then only one person will be in Heaven: Jesus.

Consider the sin of murder listed above. Paul, Moses, and David all committed murder, and yet these three men each found forgiveness. What then is John trying to communicate with these statements?

Let me suggest that John isn't trying to *threaten* us—but *comfort* us—in these passages. Notice that he uses the present tense for these sinful people—not the past tense. God will exclude those who are currently *practicing* sin—not those who *practiced* it on Earth. In other words, God will not allow people to sin in Heaven.

What a remarkable promise! What will it be like to experience relationships without the stain of sin? Even in a broken world with fractured relationships, we experience the joy of friendships, talking late into the night, only to discover that hours have sped by. Just as God originally stated, "It is not good for the man to be alone" (Gen. 2:18), innumerable people will share Heaven with us eternally. But what will it be like to experience these relationships without selfishness?—pride?—ego?—insecurity? We will be free to give and accept love to a degree we can't imagine.

No cost (Rev. 21:6)

> I will give to the one who thirsts from the spring of the water of life without cost. (Rev. 21:6)

The author of the book of Revelation also wrote the gospel of John. In this biography of Jesus' life, John records an interaction between Christ and a lonely and desperate woman. As Jesus sat with this woman around a water hole in the hot sun, he told her,

> If you knew the gift of God and who it is that asks you for a drink, you would have asked him and he would have given you living water... Whoever drinks the water I give him will never thirst. Indeed, the water I give him will become in him a spring of water welling up to eternal life. (Jn. 4:10, 14 NIV; cf. 7:37-38)

In Heaven, these promises come to their ultimate fulfillment. We will guzzle this living water, free of charge: "I will give to the one who thirsts from the spring of the water of life without cost" (Rev. 21:6). Yes, you read that right: "Without cost."

Heaven is a free gift for those who choose to accept it.

Chapter 7: What happens seconds after death?

Best-selling novels and blockbuster films about the afterlife grip our attention. Our culture simply can't shake the reality of Heaven, and many find themselves at least curious about the topic. We all seem to have questions about Heaven, and fortunately, the Bible has answers.

God will eventually restore our world to a state of perfection, but this restoration of Earth will not happen for a very long time. Where will we go in the meantime?

The Present Heaven

At death, our souls will leave our bodies and appear before God in what theologians call the Present Heaven (or the "intermediate state"). If you plan a trip to Paris, you might have a "layover" in Atlanta, but this isn't your final destination. Similarly, while we will "layover" in the Present Heaven, our final home will be the renewed Earth.[1]

Scripture uses the term "sleep" to describe death (Jn. 11:11-14; Acts 7:60; 13:36; 1 Cor. 15:51; 1 Thess. 4:13). As a result, Seventh-Day Adventists and Jehovah's Witnesses believe in "soul sleep." In this view, we will "sleep" or cease from consciousness until God raises us from the dead at the end of history. At the moment of death, do we cease to exist?

---

[1] I am indebted to Randy Alcorn for this illustration. Randy C. Alcorn, *Heaven*, 43.

Not according to the Bible. Just before he died, Jesus told one of the other crucifixion victims, "Truly I say to you, *today* you shall be with Me in Paradise" (Lk. 23:43). The thief expected Jesus to remember him in his kingdom in the distant future (v.42), but instead, Jesus promised he would enter Heaven "today."[2] Similarly, Stephen didn't pray for God to put him to sleep at death, but rather to "receive [his] spirit" (Acts 7:59).

God has taken believers to Heaven before. For instance, he took Elijah directly into Heaven (2 Kings 2:1), and later when Elijah appeared to Jesus on the Mount of Transfiguration, he was obviously conscious—hundreds of years after his death (Mt. 17:3).

Perhaps the best evidence against the notion of "soul sleep" comes from the apostle Paul. He believed that "to die is *gain*" (Phil. 1:21), and he wrote, "I desire to depart and be with Christ, which is *better by far*" (Phil. 1:23 NIV). Elsewhere, Paul wrote, "While we are *at home in the body* we are *absent from the Lord*... [I] prefer rather to be *absent from the body* and to be at *home with the Lord*" (2 Cor. 5:6, 8). Paul believed that *nothing* could separate him from the love of

---

[2] Proponents of soul sleep claim that the comma should be moved to *after* the word "today." In other words, he was saying, "Today I've got something true to tell you... You will be with me in Paradise." Yet such a reading is tortured. We don't discover Jesus ever saying this in his other usages of "truly I say to you" (*amēn soi legō*; cf. Lk. 4:24; 12:37; 18:17, 29; 21:32), even though Luke likes to use the term "today" to show immediacy (Lk. 2:11; 4:21; 5:26; 13:32–33; 22:34, 61). This is why scholar Leon Morris can write, "Today is occasionally taken with the preceding words, but there seems no reason for this. Almost all scholars agree that it refers to being in Paradise." Leon Morris, *Luke: an Introduction and Commentary* (Downers Grove, IL: InterVarsity Press, 1988), 346.

God—not even death itself (Rom. 8:38-39).[3] Heaven is a state of "rest," but it isn't a state of non-existence.

Hades: The Present Hell

Just as there is a *Present Heaven* for those who will inherit the New Heaven and Earth, Hades serves as a *Present Hell* for those who will be separated from God forever (Rev. 20:13-14; Mt. 11:23; 16:18; Lk. 16:23; Rev. 1:18).

The term "Hades" comes from two Greek root words: *a* ("not") and *idein* ("to see"). Hence "Hades" refers to being "unseen" or "invisible." The ancient Greek poet Homer used it to refer to the "abode of the dead" or the "underworld." After Homer, Greek people began using the term more generally to refer to "the grave" or "death."[4]

It bothers some people that the Bible would adopt the language of paganism to describe genuine spiritual realities. Yet this really shouldn't surprise us. Pagans used the term *theos* ("god") to describe the gods of Greece, but the New Testament authors adopted this same term to refer to the real infinite-personal God of the Bible. Even today, our English word "God" comes from the Germanic and Norse words for Pagan gods ("Gut" and "Guð"). The origin of a word is far less important than its definition and use in the present.

Those in Hades currently await their ultimate judgment from God—just as believers will await their ultimate reward. Peter writes, "The Lord knows how to rescue the

---

[3] Anthony A. Hoekema, *The Bible and the Future* (Grand Rapids, MI: William B. Eerdmans Publishing Company, 1979), 104.

[4] L. Coenen, *New International Dictionary of New Testament Theology*, 206.

godly from temptation, and to keep the unrighteous under punishment for the day of judgment" (2 pet. 2:9). When those in Hades rise from the dead, it won't be a moment of rescue—but of righteous judgment.

What can we expect in the Present Heaven?

In just three short verses, Revelation 6 tells us a great deal about the Present Heaven. John writes:

> I saw underneath the altar the souls of those who had been slain because of the word of God, and because of the testimony which they had maintained; [10] and they cried out with a loud voice, saying, "How long, O Lord, holy and true, will You refrain from judging and avenging our blood on those who dwell on the earth?" [11] And there was given to each of them a white robe; and they were told that they should rest for a little while longer, until the number of their fellow servants and their brethren who were to be killed even as they had been, would be completed also. (Rev. 6:9-11)

This passage tells us several key details about the reality of the Present Heaven:[5]

> 1. These believers in the Present Heaven are the same people they were on Earth—only made perfect (Heb. 12:23).

---

[5] I have altered and abridged the 21 point list given by Alcorn. Randy C. Alcorn, *Heaven*, 65-67.

2. They still have desires. In Heaven, we won't become braindead, emotionless, or apathetic. We'll be more engaged in God's plan than ever before.

3. They communicate directly with God. These believers ask God questions, and he gives them answers.

4. They remember their former lives on Earth — specifically the fact that they were murdered.

5. They are aware of the passage of time ("How long, O Lord?").

6. They have a deeper understanding of God's character ("O Lord, holy and true").

7. They still care for their loved ones, mentioning their "fellow servants" and "brethren" who were still on Earth.

Believers in the Present Heaven can see the events happening on Earth. This doesn't mean we will become all-knowing in Heaven, but we will be able to see at least the major events in God's plan. John later adds, "Rejoice over her, O heaven, *and you saints and apostles and prophets*, because God has pronounced judgment for you against her" (Rev. 18:20). And again, he mentions a "great multitude in heaven" rejoicing over the destruction of Babylon (Rev. 19:1).

Jesus said, "There is joy in the presence of the angels of God over one sinner who repents" (Lk. 15:10). Jesus doesn't say that the *angels* rejoice over people meeting Christ on Earth, but that rejoicing occurs *in the presence* of the angels.[6] Do

---

[6] I am indebted to Randy Alcorn for this insight. Randy C. Alcorn, *Heaven*, 71.

believers throw parties in Heaven when people come to faith in Christ? It's very likely that they do!

While several biblical texts imply that believers can witness events on Earth, this doesn't mean that we should pray directly to dead loved ones (Deut. 18:10-12; Lev. 20:6, 27; 1 Sam. 28:5-18; Isa. 8:19-20). After all, Jesus taught us to pray to our "Father who is in heaven" (Mt. 6:9)—not to dead Christians—and Paul writes that we should "let [our] requests be made known to God" (Phil. 4:6). In all the prayers recorded in Scripture, none are addressed to a dead Christian.

Erwin Lutzer explains this best when he tells the story about a little girl who prayed that Jesus would give a message to her deceased "grampa." He comments, "This little girl's theology was much better than that of millions of other people in the world. She knew that although we might pray to Jesus to get a message to grampa, we don't pray to grampa to get a message to Jesus!"[7]

Will there be sex in Heaven?

The God of the Bible is definitely *pro*-sex. He invented it. He designed it. We are the recipients of this magnificent gift. Reading the Song of Solomon in public will make most people blush. Solomon tells his lover, "You are slender like a palm tree, and your breasts are like its clusters of fruit" (Song 7:7 NLT). Then he writes, "I will climb the palm tree and take hold of its fruit" (Song 7:8 NLT). To put this in modern vernacular, Solomon is saying, "Baby, I wanna touch your melons!"

---

[7] Erwin W. Lutzer, *One Minute After You Die* (Chicago, IL: Moody Press, 1997), 65.

Solomon and his wife enjoy making love all night long (Song 2:17), and he even describes foreplay before sex (Song 2:6 NET). In the Proverbs, he writes, "As a loving hind and a graceful doe, *let her breasts satisfy you at all times*; be exhilarated always with her love" (Prov. 5:19). Clearly Solomon was thinking about sex in terms far beyond mere procreation! Here was a married man who wasn't embarrassed about his sexuality or his sex drive, preserving it for us in Scripture.

But while the Bible is clearly pro-sex, it surprises us to read this statement from Jesus: "In the resurrection they neither marry nor are given in marriage" (Mt. 22:30). If there is no marriage in Heaven, it would seem that there will not be sex either.

Some feel tremendously disappointed by the fact that we will no longer have sex in Heaven. But just imagine explaining the joy of Heaven to a five year old boy.[8] After you're finished explaining, the young boy asks, "That sounds great... but will my favorite candy be in Heaven?" You might respond by saying, "Maybe and maybe not... but who cares? You'll be in Heaven!"

Could we be like the young boy in the illustration, elevating the good pleasure of sex over the greater pleasures of being in the presence of God (Ps. 16:11)? Could we be settling for something that's *good* for something that's even *greater*? We often use the expression "better than sex" to describe food, drinks, or other exhilarating experiences. Could it be that

---

[8] I am indebted to C.S. Lewis for this illustration, though I altered it. C. S. Lewis, *Miracles: A Preliminary Study* (New York: Harper Collins, 1996), 260-261.

Heaven will be so good that sex will fade into the background?

One way to view the absence of sex in Heaven is to feel that we will miss out. Another view is that we've been missing out on the joy of Heaven all of our lives, and we'll be leaving behind something that's great in order to gain pleasure that is even greater.

Will we eat and drink in Heaven?

Remember, we will be resurrected just as Jesus was resurrected (1 Jn. 3:2). In his resurrected body, Luke records, "They gave [Jesus] a piece of a broiled fish; and He took it and ate it before them" (Lk. 24:42-43). Likewise, Jesus said, "Mark my words—I will not drink wine again until the day I drink it new with you in my Father's Kingdom" (Mt. 26:29 NLT). So if Jesus ate and drank, we will too (cf. Isa. 25:6). Of course, Christ didn't need to eat, but maybe he did so because he simply enjoyed it. In Heaven, we will eat and drink—not out of necessity—but out of sheer delight.

Will there be animals (or pets) in Heaven?

Animals existed in the Garden at the beginning of creation, so there seems to be no good reason why they won't exist in Heaven. Some Christians do not believe pets will be in Heaven,[9] while others speculate that they will.[10]

Yet it would be a shame to make this our focus. My friend works at a Christian library. One of the patrons returned a

---

[9] Tada appeals to Ecclesiastes 3:21, where Solomon asks, "Who knows that the breath of man ascends upward and the breath of the beast descends downward to the earth?" Joni Eareckson Tada, *Heaven*, 54.

[10] Hank Hanegraaff, *AfterLife*, 45. Randy C. Alcorn, *Heaven*, 397-409.

book about Heaven to the library, and my friend asked her what she thought about it. The woman said, "It was terrific... I didn't know that we will have our pets in Heaven!" My friend quickly replied, "Yeah, that's certainly possible... but did you know that *God* will be there too?"

Sure, animals (and maybe even pets) will be in Heaven. But those who make the focus of Heaven their *pets* really should evaluate their emphasis.

How old will we look in Heaven?

Will infants be perpetually three months old in Heaven? Will elderly believers remain 95 for all of eternity? Do we come back to life at the age we died, or some other age?

The Bible never directly addresses this question. Personally, I hope that Heaven will have at least some children running around. But will they stay children forever? We simply do not have enough biblical data to answer. Of course, the first humans were not born as infants; they were created as fully grown adults—at least past the point of puberty because they were married and sexually active (Gen. 1:28; 2:24).

Likewise, Jesus died in his thirties, and he was resurrected in this same age—not reverting to being a teenager or a child. So, some theologians believe we will be resurrected in the prime of life—not as infants or in old age.[11]

Still others think that if a mother loses a child early in life or in infancy, she will raise that child in Heaven. In other words, God will give back to those parents all of the

---

[11] Theologian Alister McGrath writes, "The New Jerusalem will thus be populated by men and women as they would appear at the age of 30." Alister E. McGrath, *A Brief History of Heaven* (Oxford: Blackwell Publishing, 2003), 38.

moments that were lost on Earth, and "the children will grow up with their parents."[12]

Our questions will all be answered

Most of our questions about Heaven don't come from knowing too much—but too little. Paul writes, "Now we see in a mirror dimly, but then face to face; now I know in part, but then I will know fully" (1 Cor. 13:12). Not all of our questions will be answered in this life, but we should learn to anticipate the day when they will. One of the deeply satisfying pleasures of Heaven will be to listen as God patiently answers all of our questions about this life as well as the next.

---

[12] Erwin W. Lutzer, *One Minute After You Die*, 74.

Chapter 8: Objections to eternal life

Some people can find a reason to complain—no matter what the circumstances. While the gift of Heaven is remarkable, many people remain skeptical about eternal life. Let's consider some of these key objections raised against Heaven.

Will Heaven be an eternal church service?

Many remember being dragged to church as children to sing hymns, and they wonder if Heaven will be like one of these boring services—only lasting forever! Atheist P. Z. Myers writes, "Who would want to even visit... Heaven, with all its smug and judgmental inhabitants praising God non-stop with pursed lips and suspicious eyes?"[1]

However, this objection probably says more about the baggage of contemporary church culture than it does about Heaven. While church services can be boring, Heaven will not.

Consider how people pay hundreds of dollars for front row seats to a rock concert. They do this because they love the band, enjoy the songs, and know all of the lyrics. Time seems to fly when you're enjoying yourself! Similarly, we

---

[1] P.Z. Myers, "Sunday Sacrilege: Imagine no Heaven." June 6, 2010.
http://scienceblogs.com/pharyngula/2010/06/06/sunday-sacrilege-imagine-no-he/

won't be dragged against our will to sing to God in Heaven. We'll enjoy it.

Furthermore, most of the passages about "worship services" in Heaven are actually *shouted*—not *sung* (Rev. 5:11-12; 6:1, 10; 7:10). Imagine going to a college football game when the team takes the field. Thousands of people stand and scream. You can feel the deafening noise deep in your chest and the camaraderie of cheering your team on to victory. The electricity of Heaven will be like this—only much, much more. We won't be cheering a rock singer in skinny jeans or a group of athletes in jerseys. We'll be screaming and singing to our Creator.

Singing will not be our *only* activity in Heaven. These passages are only one snapshot of Heaven. God designed humans to work and engage in productive activity (Gen. 2:15; 2:20). That's why when we're idle for too long, we get depressed, bored, or restless. We feel the need for a sense of accomplishment. According to Jesus, this inherent need will continue on into eternity. In fact, he even promised to entrust us with leadership in Heaven:

> You are a good servant. You have been faithful with the little I entrusted to you, *so you will be governor of ten cities as your reward*. (Lk. 19:17 NLT)

Heaven will be filled with activity—not passivity. Much of our joy will come from giving, serving, and leading others under God's leadership.

Won't Heaven get boring after millions of years?

Heaven will be exciting for the first few million years, *but forever?* Won't we get bored after a while? Carol Zaleski writes, "Our ancestors were afraid of Hell; we are afraid of Heaven. We think it will be boring."[2] Atheist P.Z. Myers quips, "All wishes are fulfilled, all desires achieved, we're done with everything we've ever dreamed of, making Heaven a kind of retirement home where everyone is waiting to die. Waiting forever."[3]

While this objection might be good rhetoric, Heaven will not ever be boring for one simple reason: the infinite-personal God will be there. Hanegraaff writes, "Finite creations will never come to the end of exploring the infinite Creator."[4] We will continually "know the love of Christ which surpasses knowledge" (Eph. 3:19). How long will it take for a limited being to discover and experience the love and knowledge of an infinite Being? It will take an *eternity.*

Time seems to drag the most when we're dissatisfied with our circumstances. The last hour of a work shift always seems to take the longest. But time hardly seems to drag when we're on a roller coaster or at a good party. When we're falling in love for the first time, we often say that "time flies by" or even "stands still." We don't have our eyes on the clock, because our eyes are fixed on something else—or really, *someone* else. We've never experienced what

---

[2] Carol Zaleski, "In Defense of Immortality," *First Things* 105 (August—September 2000), 42. Cited in Jerry Walls (editor), *The Oxford Handbook of Eschatology* (Oxford: Oxford UP, 2008), 389.

[3] P.Z. Myers, "Sunday Sacrilege: Imagine no Heaven."

[4] Hank Hanegraaff, *AfterLife*, 30.

it's like to be in the direct presence of God. But if the biblical text can be trusted at all, we can rest assured that it will be anything but boring.

Does focusing on Heaven make us detached from the problems here on Earth?

Perhaps you've heard the famous saying, "Some people are so heavenly minded that they are no earthly good." Many people claim that if we spend too much time focusing on another world, we will become disinterested in making an impact in this one.

But the opposite is true. The reality of eternity offers a powerful motivation to live sacrificially, one that is nonsensical to those without it.

To illustrate, imagine if you were a prisoner of war. One day, you receive word that the war is over, and your comrades will soon raid the prison, breaking everyone out. *Under these conditions, would you be more or less likely to share my limited supply of food and clean water with your fellow inmates?* Of course, you'd want to keep some to survive, but not at the expense of seeing others starve to death. On the other hand, if you didn't believe help was coming, what would motivate you to radically sacrifice your resources for others?

We need hope to endure for very long. Just imagine two men trying to survive in that prison: One knows his wife and children are alive, waiting for him after the war; while the other knows that his wife and children have been killed.

Which man do you think will have more motivation to endure his suffering?[5]

We might observe that many Christians don't live a very sacrificial lifestyle, squandering their resources on themselves. But this is exactly the point: It's only as we *reflect* on the reality of eternity that our grip loosens on our resources, and we find the freedom to love others in the short time we have left. As C.S. Lewis once wrote, "Aim at Heaven and you will get earth 'thrown in': aim at earth and you will get neither."[6]

Will we have freewill in Heaven?

God will not suddenly turn us into automatons in Heaven. Such a thought runs contrary to everything we read in Scripture regarding the high premium God places on human freedom. Yet some wonder how it could be possible to have genuine freewill, but never choose to sin. Won't we be just as vulnerable to another moral fall as the first humans in the Garden?

Not at all. In Heaven, we will have something that the first humans didn't have and probably couldn't conceive of: *The Cross*. Any time we question God's motives or character, we will see the gory wounds in Jesus' hands and feet, remembering the great price that he paid for us.

While it's logically possible that someone could rebel from God in eternity, it will never actually happen because we will never choose to do such a thing. To illustrate this, consider holding your newborn baby in your hands for the

---

[5] I am indebted to Tim Keller for this illustration.
[6] C. S. Lewis, *Mere Christianity* (New York: Harper Collins, 2001), 134.

first time. While it is logically possible for you to torture or abuse the child, you are so overwhelmed with love that you would never even think of such a thing. Similarly, but to a far greater degree, our love for Christ (or rather his love for us) will be so overwhelming that we will never rebel against him ever again.

If you grieve, does that mean you don't really believe?

Skeptics argue that grief is inconsistent with the Christian faith. If we really do believe that our loved one is in Heaven, then why do we experience grief and mourning? Atheist Ian McEwan said,

> I think people don't really believe the myths they invent. I've been to many funerals in which the priest has spoken of an afterlife and even the people who are there are sobbing profusely. They don't *really* think they're gonna meet their loved one in five years' time.[7]

This criticism doesn't carry weight. For one, Jesus cried at the funeral of a close friend (Jn. 11:33-35), and he grieved the loss of John the Baptist (Mt. 14:13-14). Was Jesus a phony who didn't really believe in God or the afterlife? Can we really take such an objection seriously?

In fact, as we read through our Bibles, we discover that fervent believers in God still passionately grieved the loss of loved ones:

---

[7] Richard Dawkins and Lawrence Krauss, *The Unbelievers*. December, 2013.

Jacob mourned when he heard Joseph had died (Gen. 37:34-35).

David hysterically mourned the death of his newborn son—even though he had a sincere faith that he would see him again (2 Sam. 12:15-18). Additionally, David wept over the death of Amnon (2 Sam. 13:37), Absalom (2 Sam. 18:33), King Saul, and his friend Jonathan (2 Sam. 1:11-12).

Jesus was "a man of sorrows and acquainted with grief" (Isa. 53:3).

"Godly men" openly wept at the death of Stephen (Acts 8:2 NIV).

Paul worried about losing his dear friend Epaphroditus, because this would cause him "sorrow upon sorrow" (Phil. 2:27).

There is nothing wrong (at all!) in grieving the loss of our loved ones, even if we carry the conviction that they are in Heaven. We don't grieve over the fact that our loved one is in Heaven which is "better by far" (Phil. 1:23 NIV). Instead, we grieve because we are *currently separated* from them. The person we saw every day for years is gone, and it hurts to be torn apart.

Years ago, dear friends of ours moved overseas. Even though we believed we'd see them again, my wife still went through a period of intense grief at losing one of her closest friends to the other side of the world. Even though she could Skype once a week and visit now and then, the pain of separation was profound. To a greater degree, losing a loved one in death is a severe and sudden separation. It's possible to carry the conviction that we'll see them again, while also suffering from the separation.

Of course, while grief affects all people, Christians have an ability to quietly anchor their hope in Heaven. They certainly do grieve, but they don't grieve the same way. As Paul writes, we should "not grieve like people who have no hope" (1 Thess. 4:13 NLT).

How can we be resurrected if our bodies have been completely destroyed?

Like the Sadducees who denied the resurrection in Jesus' day (Mt. 22:23ff), many skeptics wonder how the resurrection of the dead can be possible when some humans have been cremated or cannibalized (cf. 1 Cor. 15:35-36). Since their bodies have been utterly annihilated, how could they possibly be resurrected in the future?

Of course, this objection really shows a low view of God's power. It resembles the King in the nursery rhyme "Humpty Dumpty," rather than the God of the Bible. If God can turn water into wine or create the entire universe from nothing, why would we doubt his power in raising us from the dead? As an all-powerful and all-knowing being, God has the ability to regenerate every last cell in our bodies — even if they have been scattered across the globe.

Furthermore, the *molecules* in my body are not essentially *me*. The molecules constantly change, but I remain the same. I am not the same *physical* person that I was last year or last decade. My cells die and regenerate; skin flakes off; yet I am still *myself*. Regardless of the physical composition of our bodies (which never stays the same—not even now), when

Christ raises us from the dead, we will exist in a new imperishable body.

Just wait and see

Our speculations about eternity might seem sensible now, but how horrible to prejudge a place we've never been. Seconds after death, our skepticism about Heaven will quickly evaporate. The raw experience of standing in the presence of God will eclipse any cynicism that seemed so justified before. One day, all of our theology will be corrected in a moment of time.

Chapter 9: Living with the reality of eternity

Very few live with the reality of eternity, convincing themselves that they need to grasp at whatever pleasure, entertainment, and stimulation they can before it's too late. Robbed of eternity, they restlessly fill their lives with whatever experiences they can before the clock runs out.

Sadly, this lack of an emphasis on eternity can even be found in Christian circles. In his 800 page book on *Systematic Theology*, theologian Louis Berkhof spends just *four paragraphs* explaining the reality of Heaven. Most Christians don't think of Heaven too much, but too little.

This must be why the Bible instructs us to think about the reality of Heaven. Paul writes, "Keep seeking the things above, where Christ is" (Col. 3:1) The Greek term for "seek" here means "to seek information, investigate, examine, consider, deliberate."[1] The Bible uses this word to describe the way Jesus would "seek" to save sinners (Lk. 19:10), or how Herod's men "sought" to kill Jesus as an infant (Mt. 2:20). According to Scripture, we should think about Heaven actively, deliberately, and repeatedly.

Many Christians focus too much on the benefits of following Christ in this life, rather than the next. We hear many Bible teachings about how following Christ will be good for our happiness and satisfaction. While this is certainly true (Mk.

---

[1] W. Arndt (et al.), *A Greek-English Lexicon of the New Testament and Other Early Christian Literature*. 3rd ed. (Chicago: University of Chicago Press, 2000), 428.

10:29-30; Jn. 13:17; Acts 20:35), the Bible emphasizes the rewards of the next life as our primary motivation.

In fact, a mind focused on eternity has the ability to radically change our lives.

Eternity reminds us that people are the only lasting commodity

At the moment of death, all of our financial investments, stocks, and assets immediately lose value. No matter how we invest our money, we all become bankrupt the instant we leave this world. The old proverb remains true: *There are no trailers attached to hearses.* As Paul writes, "We have brought nothing into the world, so we cannot take anything out of it either" (1 Tim. 6:7).

A man once stood at the funeral of a rich financier as he was being lowered in the ground. Curious about his net worth, the man meekly whispered to his accountant, "How much did he leave?"

The accountant aptly said, "He left *all of it!*"

While we can't bring possessions into eternity, we can transfer our wealth into an eternal economy. Jesus spoke of the "true riches" that will never fade (Lk. 16:11). He taught,

> Store up for yourselves treasures in heaven, where neither moth nor rust destroys, and where thieves do not break in or steal. (Mt. 6:20)

> Make yourselves money belts which do not wear out, an unfailing treasure in heaven, where no thief comes near nor moth destroys. (Lk. 12:33)

When Paul praised the Philippians for their generosity, he reminded them,

> [I do not] seek the [financial] gift itself, but I seek for the profit which increases to your account. (Phil. 4:17)

By giving their money generously to the cause of Christ, Paul wrote that wealthy Christians could invest in eternal treasures:

> [Generous Christians will be] storing up for themselves the treasure of a good foundation for the future, so that they may take hold of that which is life indeed. (1 Tim. 6:19)

This is the language of banking and accounting (e.g., "store up" "treasures" "money belts" "increases to your account"). No other investment compares to investing in eternity. Alcorn writes, "Jesus isn't saying it's wrong to invest. He's saying, 'Don't make a stupid investment, make a smart one.'"[2] As Jim Elliot famously said, "He is no fool who gives what he cannot keep, to gain what he cannot lose."[3]

Imagine if you had an enormous amount of Confederate money in 1864, what would you do with it?[4] Surely you'd try and transfer it into real U.S. currency, because your money would be worth less than toilet paper relativity soon. Similarly, our spiritual war will soon be over too (either when we die or when Christ returns), and we will be stuck

---

[2] Randy C. Alcorn, *Money, Possessions, and Eternity* (Wheaton, IL: Tyndale House, 2003), 94.

[3] Jim Elliot, *Journal Entry*. October 28, 1949.

[4] Randy C. Alcorn, *Money, Possessions, and Eternity*, 100.

with useless green pieces of paper in our bank accounts that won't be worth anything for the rest of eternity.

Why would we ever invest in something that will suddenly disappear? Imagine if a close friend told you to invest in Blockbuster video rental months before it went out of business. This would be a foolish investment, right? Yet many people make exactly the same mistake—only to a much larger degree. Instead of forfeiting our money *temporarily*, they forfeit it *eternally*.

Francis Schaeffer once wrote of those Christians who were what he called "practical atheists."[5] A practical atheist, says Schaeffer, is a Christian who lives practically as if God and eternal life do not exist. Instead of living for eternity, most people "have only two values—personal peace and affluence."[6] As believers, do we live as though God and eternity exist? Sadly, Schaeffer's assessment still rings true today. Many Christians can accurately explain the truths of Christ and eternity—yet they live as though neither are true.

God's economy values people as the central, precious commodity—only people will continue into eternity. Most of our reward in Heaven will be the relationships that come with us. Paul writes,

> Who is our hope or joy or crown of exultation? Is it not even you, in the presence of our Lord Jesus at

---

[5] Actually, Schaeffer used the term "practical materialists." However, few lay people use the term "materialist" to refer to a philosophical naturalist. Therefore, for clarity and communication, I use the term "atheist." Francis A. Schaeffer, *The Complete Works of Francis A. Schaeffer*. Volume Three. (Wheaton, IL: Crossway Books, 1985), 182.

[6] Francis A. Schaeffer, *The Complete Works of Francis A. Schaeffer*, 182.

> His coming? For you are our glory and joy. (1 Thess.
> 2:19-20; cf. Phil. 4:1)

Notice that our reward is not a *what* but a *who*. When we get to Heaven, nothing will follow us but those people who met Christ. Our possessions will perish, but people will persist.

John writes that in Heaven "the street of the city was pure gold" (Rev. 21:21). This side of eternity, gold is a precious commodity. We stockpile it behind bank vaults and shoot someone on sight for trying to steal it. On the other side of eternity, gold will be worth less than tar or asphalt. In fact, we'll be paving our streets with it.

Eternity reminds us why temporal pursuits never truly satisfy

Money brings happiness on some level, but such happiness is frivolously fleeting. Like grabbing a fistful of Jell-O, the harder you squeeze, the more it slips through your fingers. Secular researchers agree. According to one study, lottery winners were temporarily elated to win the jackpot, but they returned to their former emotional state only *eight weeks* afterward.[7] Psychologist Tim Kasser writes,

> Evidence suggests that, beyond having enough
> money to meet our basic needs for food, shelter, and
> the like, attaining wealth, possessions, and status
> *does not yield long-term increases in our happiness or*
> *well-being.* Even the successful pursuit of

---

[7] P. Brickman (et al.), "Lottery winners and accident victims: Is happiness relative?" *Journal of Personality and Social Psychology.* 36, 1978. 917-27.

materialistic ideals typically turns out to be *empty and unsatisfying*.[8]

Psychologists Richard Ryan and Edward Deci write,

> The more people focus on financial and materialistic goals, the lower their well-being... Money does not appear to be a reliable route to either happiness or wellbeing... There appear to be many risks to poverty but few benefits to wealth when it comes to well-being.[9]

These secular researchers confirm what the Bible has taught all along: Once our needs are met (1 Tim. 6:8), additional wealth doesn't make us happy. As Paul writes,

> People who want to get rich fall into temptation and a trap and into many foolish and harmful desires that plunge men into ruin and destruction. [10] For the love of money is a root of all kinds of evil. Some people, eager for money, have wandered from the faith and pierced themselves with many griefs. (1 Tim. 6:9-10)

Jesus taught, "Where your treasure is, there your heart will be also" (Mt. 6:21). If our money goes into our houses or cars, then our emotional lives will be absorbed in those things. If we give our money over to the cause of Christ, we will become emotional about that as well. It's no wonder that Jesus' teaching on the love of wealth (Mt. 6:21-24) was immediately followed by a teaching on anxiety (Mt. 6:25-34).

---

[8] Emphasis mine. Tim Kasser, *The High Price of Materialism* (Cambridge, MA: MIT, 2002), 43.

[9] Richard M. Ryan and Edward L. Deci. "On Happiness and Human Potentials: A Review of Research on Hedonic and Eudaimonic Well-Being." *Annual Review of Psychology*. 2001. 153-154.

Eternity reminds us that our suffering has purpose

In "The Sound of Thunder" (1952), science fiction author Ray Bradbury tells the short story of a time traveler who hunts dinosaurs in the distant past. When he returns to the future, he discovers a drastically different world: people speak differently and a fascist dictator has been elected president. As the time traveler searches for an explanation for what happened, he looks under his boot to discover he had stepped on a butterfly in the past. That one seemingly insignificant act radically changed the course of human history!

Could we be in the same situation today? While our suffering might seem pointless in this life, it can multiply in significance in eternity.

When he was an infant, I took my son to get his vaccination shots at the doctor's office. I'll never forget how he went from smiling and cooing in the waiting room to screaming like a heavy metal singer the second the first needle punctured his skin. He looked at me with tears in his eyes, as if to say, *"How could you do this to me? I thought you loved me! Why would you put me through this?!"*

Of course, I knew better than my newborn son. At his age and mental development, he couldn't comprehend terms like "Hepatitis B," "Influenza," or "Polio." I couldn't explain why we were causing him pain. But as a loving father, I put him through this pain for a greater purpose.

As I reflect on this event, I begin to wonder: *If I can know something about my son's suffering that he cannot understand, is it possible (or even probable) that God knows something about my suffering that I cannot fathom?* I might feel infinitely more intelligent than my newborn son, but I must look no more intelligent than a termite compared to God! We're too limited to see how God will use our suffering in light of eternity. One of the great comforts of Heaven will be understanding why God permitted the suffering in our lives and how he used it to impact others for eternity.

Eternity reminds us to be faithful with the small stuff

Have you ever heard of Edward Kimball?

Probably not. He was a "nobody." He taught a small Sunday school class in the 1800s. One day, Kimball felt a burden to share his faith with one of the young men in his class. He visited the boy at the shoe shop where he worked. After he left the store, he didn't feel like he had any sort of impact on the kid…

But he did.

That young man's name was Dwight Moody, who later shared his faith over two continents, bringing thousands to faith in Jesus. He also started Moody Bible Institute.

While Moody had a large impact for Christ, he specifically inspired a man by the name of Frederic Meyer to give his life to Christ. Meyer became a preacher, and one day while preaching, Wilbur Chapman heard him say: "If you are not willing to give up everything for Christ, are you willing to be made willing?" Wilbur Chapman dedicated his life to Christ shortly thereafter.

Chapman took a baseball player by the name of Billy Sunday under his wing, and taught him how to teach the

Bible and lead others for Christ. Billy Sunday took over his Christian organization and sparked a large revival. He also funded a Bible teacher named Mordecai Ham to teach the young people of Charlotte, North Carolina in 1932.

One night, a lanky, sandy blonde 16-year-old kid came to hear Mordecai Ham teach the Bible, and he gave his life to Christ too.

That young man's name was Billy Graham.

Today, Billy Graham has shared Jesus' message of love and forgiveness with over 2.2 billion people. Edward Kimball died without knowing any of this, but years later, we can see his spiritual legacy.[10]

We often don't feel like we have much to offer God in the way of our gifts or abilities. But like the young boy who put his "five loaves and two fish" in the hands of Jesus, we will discover in eternity just how much God could do with our meager efforts.

Eternity reminds us that we will all give an account of our lives someday

Christians will never know what it's like to experience God's judgment, but we will know what it's like to have our lives evaluated by God. The Bible teaches that God will "test the quality of each man's work" (1 Cor. 3:13). The purpose of this assessment is not punishment—but reward (v.14). Paul explicitly writes, "If any man's work is burned up, he will suffer loss; *but he himself will be saved*" (v.15). So nobody at this judgment is condemned.

---

[10] Waylon Moore, *Multiplying Disciples* (Colorado Springs, CO: NavPress, 1981), 15-16.

Theologians call this the *bema seat judgment*. Paul writes, "We must all appear before the judgment seat [*bema*] of Christ" (2 Cor. 5:10; cf. Rom. 14:10). As Jesus promised, "I am coming quickly, and My reward is with Me, to render to every man according to what he has done" (Rev. 22:12).

The New Testament authors use the word "crown" to describe our reward, which was an "award or prize for exceptional service or conduct."[11] In ancient times, athletes would gain a "crown" if they won their race—almost like getting a gold, silver, or bronze medal today.[12] Poor athletes weren't punished; they simply forfeited reward. Similarly, this judgment for reward isn't a *threat*, but an *opportunity* to receive rewards. James (Jas. 1:12), Paul (1 Cor. 9:25; 2 Tim. 4:8), Peter (1 Pet. 5:4), and John (Rev. 2:10) all wrote about this crown of reward, so it must have been motivating to Jesus' closest followers.

At the end of Steven Spielberg's movie *Schindler's List* (1993), Oskar Schindler (Liam Neeson) stands in front of 1,100 Jewish refugees he saved from Hitler's Holocaust. He weeps as he explains his deep regret over the people he could've saved from the concentration camps.

> Oskar Schindler: "I could have gotten more out. I could have gotten more."
>
> Itzhak Stern: "Oscar, there are 1,100 people who are alive, because of you... Look at them!"

---

11 W. Arndt (et al.), *A Greek-English Lexicon of the New Testament and Other Early Christian Literature*, 944.

12 Colin J. Hemer, *New International Dictionary of New Testament Theology*, 405.

Oskar Schindler: "If I had made more money... I threw away so much money. You have no idea. If I just..."

Itzhak Stern: "There will be generations of people because of what you did."

Oskar Schindler: "I didn't do enough."

[Stern looks directly into Schindler's eyes]

Itzhak Stern: "You did so much."

Oskar Schindler: "This car... Why did I keep the car? Ten people right there. Ten people. This pin... Two people... This is gold... Two more people... He would have given me two more. At least one... I could have gotten one more person *[begins weeping]*... and I didn't." *[Itzhak Stern hugs Schindler, as he falls to the ground weeping]*

Will this dramatic scene be similar to the reward seat of Christ? No wonder Paul writes that some will "suffer loss" (1 Cor. 3:15). Like a rich investor reading about the stock market during the Great Depression, all of our financial investments will be swept away. All that will remain is our investment in the cause of Christ.

At the same time, we might picture Itzhak Stern as playing the role of Christ, comforting us during our deep regret. As we condemn ourselves, we might picture Christ saying: "There are so many people here because of you... There will be generations of people because of what you did... You did so much." In other words, our regret will be tempered by the love and grace of God, and Jesus will find something to praise in every single Christian (1 Cor. 4:5).

I think about this day of reward often. What will my reward look like? Whose rewards will be surprising? Those people who were "out front" in the eyes of everyone will likely step to the back. Other silent servants of the Lord will likely step forward to receive the praise they rightly deserve (Mt. 20:16). It's very likely that we'll be surprised at how generously God will reward his followers (Mt. 25:37).

Are eternal rewards selfish?

Some people believe that living for eternal rewards is selfish, but this is not the case. Not everything that is in our *self-interest* is necessarily *selfish*. Breathing or drinking water is in our self-interest, but not selfish. Desiring to be married or have children is in our self-interest, but these are not selfish desires. Since the rewards of Heaven center on people, rather than possessions, this desire is not *selfish*—but *selfless*.

In his window into Heaven, John sees the twenty four elders throwing their crowns before the throne in front of Jesus. Could it be that our crowns will be something we can give back to Christ in the end? Maybe our rewards are given to us, so that we have something to offer Christ when we stand before him.

God sees our motives for serving him and others (1 Cor. 4:5). If our motive is to glorify ourselves, we will receive no reward (Mt. 6:16, 18). Rather than seeing our rewards as a *competition* with others, we will only get them through *cooperation* with God and other Christians (Heb. 10:24-25).

Can we lose eternal rewards?

Some Christian teachers believe that our rewards in Heaven are certain once we receive them through faith. If we wander from our faith later, these rewards will still be given to us.

Another way of looking at our reward would be that God doesn't merely look at rewarding *individual acts* of faith, but rather *our entire life* of faith. If we do not "run the race" strong until the end, we could lose our rewards because we dishonored Christ later in life.

This would make sense of why perseverance is so important. As John writes, "Watch yourselves, that you *do not lose what we have accomplished*, but that you may receive a *full* reward" (2 Jn. 8). The author of Hebrews encourages us, "Do not throw away your confidence, which has a great reward" (Heb. 10:35).

What will you regret in eternity?

Our lives could end at any hour or any day, and then...? That's it. We had one shot to make it count for eternity—one life to make an impact for Christ.

The average American lives about 78 years on Earth. While that might seem like a long time, the Bible describes that as "a vapor that appears for a little while and then vanishes away" or like "a breath" compared to eternity (Jas. 4:14; Ps. 39:5 NIV). It's amazing how true that description feels the older we get. You blink, and you've got a mortgage. You blink again, and you've got kids growing up. Time flies by so quickly, and we can't get it back.

Don't waste your life!

It's gone so fast—and then—that's it. As Paul writes, "Be careful how you live. Don't live like fools, but like those who are wise. Make the most of every opportunity" (Eph. 5:15-16 NLT; cf. Col. 4:5). Or as Moses writes, "Teach us to realize the brevity of life, so that we may grow in wisdom" (Ps. 90:12 NLT).

God wants to reveal the reality of Heaven to you. Paul writes, "I pray that the eyes of your heart may be enlightened, so that you will know what is the hope of His calling, what are the riches of the glory of His inheritance in the saints" (Eph. 1:18). I hope God may have used this little book to help you see Heaven more clearly. Like smelling Thanksgiving dinner from the kitchen, I pray you would learn to anticipate what it will be like to live with your Creator…

Forever.